THE STORY OF ALBERT EINSTEIN

Other books by the author

FUN WITH BALLET

FUN WITH COOKING

In collaboration with
Ira M. Freeman:

FUN WITH ASTRONOMY

FUN WITH YOUR CAMERA

FUN WITH CHEMISTRY

FUN WITH FIGURES

FUN WITH SCIENCE

YOUR WONDERFUL WORLD OF SCIENCE

THE STORY OF ALBERT EINSTEIN

The scientist who searched out the secrets of the universe

MAE BLACKER FREEMAN

RANDOM HOUSE NEW YORK

Ninth Printing

 PUBLISHED IN NEW YORK BY RANDOM HOUSE, INC., AND SIMULTANEOUSLY IN TORONTO, CANADA, BY RANDOM HOUSE OF CANADA, LIMITED.
LIBRARY OF CONGRESS CATALOG CARD NUMBER: 58–6197
MANUFACTURED IN THE UNITED STATES OF AMERICA
BY H. WOLFF, NEW YORK

For checking the accuracy of German historical events, the author's thanks to Louis L. Snyder, Professor of History at the City College of New York.

CONTENTS

THE STORY OF ALBERT EINSTEIN

1. *Slow Little Boy*

"This boy is stupid!" The teacher in the primary class pointed to the youngster who sat quietly in his seat, hands folded in his lap. "He cannot learn the simplest things. Look at him!"

The whole class turned to stare at Albert Einstein. Some of the bigger boys snickered. The teacher went on, "Albert, I asked you a question. Please answer at once!"

Albert did not move, or make any sign that he had heard. It seemed almost as though the teacher were talking to another boy.

Silence was heavy in the classroom. It was a long room, cold, and lighted by gray daylight that filtered in through the many-paned windows high on one wall. The boys were excited. The Einstein boy was going to be punished again, they thought, and they were glad because they did not like Albert. Anyway, it gave them a little recess from work.

The teacher was a heavy man with a thick neck and a small head which looked even smaller because all his hair was shaved off. He stood stiff and straight, and his commands to Albert were barked. "Stand! March! Out into the hall. And stay there until noontime."

Albert was relieved. This was better than a caning. It was very cold out in the hall and tiring to stand there for two hours. But it was an improvement over remaining in the classroom, trying to answer questions that seemed silly and useless.

Albert Einstein was never deliberately disobedient. He simply could not answer quickly.

Everything he said was first very carefully thought over in his mind, and this took time. The teacher was always impatient and seemed more interested in sharp, quick answers than in thoughtful ones. But talking was very difficult for little Albert and his words came only slowly and clumsily.

The school was in a suburb of the city of Munich, in Germany. Albert had been born six years before, on March 14, 1879, in a city called Ulm, eighty-five miles to the west of Munich. His parents had moved to the larger city when he was a year old.

Munich is in a southern section of Germany called Bavaria. For a thousand years, Bavaria had been an independent state with its own king. A few years before Albert was born, Bavaria gave up her independence and joined Prussia and other German states as a part of the new German empire.

Prussia's statesman-leader, Otto von Bismarck, was called the "blood-and-iron Chancellor" because he believed in a strong, powerful government and distrusted democracy. He forced the easy-going Bavarians to accept the Prussian way of life: discipline, obedience, absolute respect for authority. Under the new system, the schools were run like military machines. The teachers were like sergeants and the discipline was as strict as in an army barracks.

And so Albert stood in the cold, drafty hall. He could hear the boys in the room jumping smartly to their feet as they snapped out answers to the sharp questions of the teacher.

How good it was to get home! Things were different there. Albert's four-year-old sister Maya welcomed him with a hug, and his mother served him a warm meal in the large, comfortable, old-fashioned kitchen. The house was a pleasant one with a charming garden all around it. To the boy, it seemed a wonderful place after a day in the prison-like school.

Hermann and Pauline Einstein loved their

son dearly. They were very patient with his slowness, although sometimes they worried secretly about him. He had been slow in learning to talk, and he was not interested in the things that delighted most youngsters. He was a sober child and preferred to be off by himself when the other children were romping in the garden.

It was a comfortable life at home with a loving family. The Einsteins had many relatives and the house was always filled with visiting aunts and uncles and cousins. They often took week-end trips to the nearby mountains and went for outings on the Bavarian lakes. Sometimes they would stop at little country inns where Albert would order his favorite treat, pork sausages.

Albert enjoyed the excursions, most of all because he could be out in the countryside which he loved. He was happy when he could stroll along the paths of friendly woods, with the sunlight coming down in patchwork designs through the trees. Sometimes he would pick a single leaf from a tree and marvel at its tiny veins and wonderful structure. He would sit motionless for a long time, gazing at the little ripples of water on the surface of a lake, and at night he would watch the stars in the dark sky.

"Albert is so solemn," Uncle Rudy remarked one day as they were picnicking on the banks of the Isar River. "See how all the other youngsters laugh and play and tease each other. My little Elsa is just his age and she is so merry. But not Albert. He just sits and looks off across the lake."

Pauline Einstein, as always, was quick to defend her son. "He's quiet because he's thinking. Wait and see, he'll be a professor some day!"

Uncle Rudy laughed good-naturedly. A professor! What a joke! Only the brightest students could ever hope to reach such an honored position. But he could not blame Pauline for trying to cover up for the dullness of her son. Families must cling together and protect each other, and they all loved little Albert even though they privately feared he was retarded and would never be able to get along as well as other children.

Toys did not interest the quiet boy. While Maya played happily with dolls, little wagons, a pail and shovel, her brother would disappear silently and creep off into the bushes in a far corner of the garden. There he would crouch for a long time, fingering some pretty leaves or staring at the scurrying ants.

Whenever Albert was ill, his parents worried about him more than ever. They could give him medicine to bring down his fever or cure his cold, but they could not find anything to bring a sparkle into his tired eyes as he lay in bed. He did not complain, and seemed quite content to lie back on his pillows, staring out of the big window at the garden. They did what they could to entertain him.

One day when Albert was in bed recovering from a cold, his father went into town on business. In a store window, he noticed a small compass. "Ah, here's something that might interest Albert," thought Mr. Einstein. "Perhaps the little box with the jiggling needle will capture his attention for a while."

Mr. Einstein brought the compass home. "See what I have for you, my boy. A mysterious box with a magic needle. Look! Turn the box any way you like. Still the stubborn needle points only *that* way."

Albert took the box and placed it on his palm. He turned it one way, then the other. Always the needle returned gently to point in the same direction as before. Mr. Einstein was happy to see his son so taken with the toy.

"Papa, what makes the needle always point one way?"

"Well, you wouldn't understand that. It's the magnetism of the earth that is pulling it back."

"Mag–mag–what?" For a boy who found speech difficult, the long word was impossible.

"It doesn't matter at all," said his father kindly.

"It's just an unseen force that has a fancy name. Play with your toy and enjoy it."

"But papa, *why* does the needle do this?"

Mr. Einstein was already halfway down the stairs. "Ask Uncle Jake," he called over his shoulder. "He'll tell you."

Uncle Jake was Mr. Einstein's brother and they were in business together. They had a small electrical shop. Hermann Einstein was in charge of the work, while Jacob Einstein, who was a trained engineer, was in charge of the technical operations. It was Uncle Jake who was most patient in answering the many "why's" that Albert was always asking.

Albert lay in bed with the compass. It fascinated him for hours. Slowly, slowly he turned it. He tapped it. He slanted it. He held it upside down. No matter what he did, as soon as the needle was free to turn it swung around to point north.

Albert's thoughts whirled, and he was thrilled and excited. For the first time, he sensed that there were things in nature that could not be seen, could not be touched—could hardly be imagined. That needle was being coaxed to move by something out in space. And space was empty! His own Uncle Jake had said so. But then, space could not be empty if it had a force that could pull a compass needle.

He lay motionless for a long time. His mother came in and was startled. The boy's eyes were too bright and his cheeks were flushed. She made him give up the toy and settle down for a nap, but he did not fall asleep for a long time. And his compass became his dearest and most fascinating possession. It was his introduction to the world of science.

In spite of Uncle Jake's sympathetic help and his family's loving care, Albert Einstein continued to do badly in school. He could not say anything until he had thought long and seriously. By that time everyone had lost patience and the classwork had moved on.

When he was nine years old and in the highest grade of the elementary school, he would not say a word until it was absolutely correct. Even if it meant a thrashing, Albert would not give a false or misleading answer. This earned him the nickname of "Honest John" from his sneering fellow students, who did not hesitate to say whatever was necessary to get themselves out of trouble.

When he was ten, the boy entered Luitpold Gymnasium. In Germany, *Gymnasium* is the name for a preparatory school, and every boy who hoped to have any sort of career had to have a diploma from such a place so that he could enter a university.

It was with great misgivings that the Einsteins saw their son start his work at Luitpold. Their hearts were heavy because he had come from elementary school at the foot of his class, and was generally known as a slow and dull student.

This was Albert Einstein, who became one of the greatest scientists who ever lived.

2. *School Struggles*

Albert Einstein became a very famous man. He was followed by reporters wherever he went, and his face became familiar all over the world. He was the honored guest of royalty. Crowds rioted trying to catch a glimpse of him when he passed through a city. In his later years, there were times when he had to have a bodyguard to protect him from overeager and overcurious persons who would try to tear a button from his coat or grab his scarf to keep as a souvenir.

One day a great throng of people came to watch Einstein arrive at a railroad station. A man and his young son stood tightly pressed in a favorable spot at the front of the crowd. The two joined in the applause that welcomed the slightly stooped gentleman with the great mane of white hair. Afterward, the father turned to his son and said, "Never forget this, my boy. You have just seen the man with the greatest mind in all history."

That was how people felt about Albert Einstein. Yet it was amazing that his fame came about because of some new scientific ideas that very few people in the world could understand. This was the very thing that fascinated people so much. His work was in the field of physics, which is the branch of science that studies what *matter* is and how it acts.

Everything in the universe is made of matter—metals, people, water, air—even the moon, sun and stars. Einstein had such remarkable new ideas about these things that all other scientists looked upon him as a mental giant. Everywhere, he was greatly honored and respected simply because of his rare thinking ability. This quiet, modest scientist captured the hearts of the world.

But people cannot foresee future happenings. There was no magic way of knowing that the absent-minded Einstein boy was ever going to amount to anything. At the Luitpold Gymnasium, his quiet dreaminess was put down as sheer dullness. At home, his desire to go off quietly alone was regarded as unsociable.

School became more and more difficult for Albert. He had to learn Latin and Greek, and he had neither the tongue to speak a foreign language nor the will to memorize grammar. He began to despise the constant drilling which was used for teaching the boys. Write the rule over and over, repeat it hundreds of times. The more it was forced on him, the more resistant he became, and his mind would not accept it.

He was not much better with history. He wondered why he should have to memorize so many dates. It seemed silly, because all the dates were printed in the book where he could find them if he ever needed such information.

In all his subjects, he irritated his teachers by wanting to know why. . . . Why was this? . . . Why was that? The teacher would glare at him and roar, "Never mind why! Just answer!" His probing questions were embarrassing and disturbing to them. Often there *were* no answers. Or at least if there were, the teachers did not know them.

Uncle Jake did his best to help. When Albert asked, "What is algebra?" Uncle Jake answered, "Algebra is a jolly science. We go hunting for a little animal whose name we do not know, so we call it *x*. When we bag our game, we pounce on it and give it its right name." The subject fascinated Albert and he was able to understand it when other boys were still struggling with simple addition.

Then Albert Einstein discovered reading. In elementary school, the matter of fitting letters together to make words had been a laborious task. Now in the *Gymnasium* he realized that the words fitted wonderfully together and had special meanings. They made the beautiful poetry of Goethe and Schiller. They could tell him things he wanted to know. He could find the answers to his questions without risking the anger of his teachers.

As each year went by he read more and more. He discovered a series of books called "Bernstein's Popular Books on Natural Science." They told about animals, plants, clouds, meteors, volcanoes; they touched lightly on many scientific subjects, and Albert absorbed them all. In one of the upper classrooms, he found a textbook on geometry. In two weeks he had mastered the subject and worked all the problems accurately. He never forgot the pleasure and excitement this book brought him.

Music gave him pleasure, too. All his young life he heard the works of Bach and Beethoven and Mozart. His mother was a lover of music and every week a group of amateur musicians gathered to play in their home. Albert would hide under the dining-room table or behind the drapes to listen until he was discovered and sent to bed.

When he was six, Mrs. Einstein bought him his own violin and sent him to music classes. But he did not do well. He had no patience for playing scales over and over, or for long hours of practice. This was not music to him. Music was the flowing beauty of Mozart or the stirring chords of Bach.

All through his years at the *Gymnasium*, Albert Einstein stumbled along. He made no impression on either his teachers or his schoolmates. No one had any clue that this young boy was developing into a great scientist.

Albert's only happy experiences at the *Gymnasium* were in the classes of Professor Ruess, who taught classical literature. The boy always remembered with gratitude the professor who aroused in him a keen interest in the world of books. Some years later, when Einstein was already becoming well known, he happened to be traveling through Munich again and decided to visit Professor Ruess to thank him for the happy hours in class. When the Professor opened the door, he did not recognize the young man standing there.

"I was once your student," said Albert Einstein. "Do you remember me?"

Professor Ruess stared with suspicion at the smiling young man whom he did not recognize at all. What was he doing here? Probably wanted to borrow money.

As quickly as he could, the Professor closed the door against his visitor, and sadly the gentle young man with the greatest mind in the world turned around and walked away.

In Albert Einstein's last year at the *Gymnasium*, the family suffered a blow—the electrical shop failed. Everyone was upset and there was much family discussion. It was decided to sell the house and move to Milan, Italy, where there were relatives who would help the Einsteins become established in a new business.

"But what shall we do about Albert?" his mother worried. "He is only fifteen and must continue his work at the *Gymnasium* until he can get a diploma."

Mr. Einstein paced the floor. "Yes, what shall we do about our boy? Maya is younger, the change will not affect her too much. But Albert . . ." He glanced anxiously at his wife. They knew without speaking of it that their son's work in school was deficient and that a change at this time might upset him beyond help.

Mrs. Einstein loved her boy and wanted him with her. But she knew what was best for him. "We will leave him here," she said determinedly. "He can join us in Milan as soon as he graduates."

So it was arranged. Albert was installed in a Munich boarding house and he continued his last year at the *Gymnasium* away from his family.

For several months he plodded along. He disliked school more than ever and grew increasingly unhappy. Now he did not even have the comfort and solace of his pleasant home and loving family. More than ever he was in trouble with his teachers. One day, one of them summoned him and said: "Einstein, I must insist that you stop asking questions in my classes. I have no answers for them, and the students are losing their respect for me. It seems to me that, if you should decide to leave this school, it might be a very good idea."

This was the final blow. Albert Einstein could not go on. He persuaded his doctor to give him a note saying that he was in poor health and needed a rest. All too readily, the school officials granted him a leave of absence and very soon after that the boy was on a train for Milan.

3. Holiday in Italy

Beautiful Italy! Bright, sparkling Italy, where the blue of the sky seemed so brilliant, and where sunshine seemed to lie on everything like liquid gold. Even as he arrived, Albert felt the wonderful charm and warmth of the country. Almost at once the dreary discontent of the past six months in Munich began to disappear.

His family welcomed him with joy. His mother hugged him tightly and then drew back to study him. She was not pleased with what she saw. He had lost weight and was quite pale, and the lids of his usually alert eyes seemed heavy, as though they were reluctant to open wide on any unpleasantness.

"*Ach*, you are so thin, *mein Albertl*," and she sighed. She always called him by this name which meant "dear little Albert" and it sounded like "All-bettle" when she said it. "But we will soon fix that, now that you are home again. Can you guess what you will have for dinner this very night?"

A roguish twinkle came into Albert's eyes. "Hummingbirds' eggs in wine sauce?"

"Ho! Such an idea. No! You are to have a big, steaming bowl of thick lentil soup, crowded with your favorite sausages." Mrs. Einstein was a good housewife and was quite sure that all her son needed were some rich, heavy German meals to build him up.

Albert smiled. It was good to be back with his family. Another boy might have shouted with joy and raced to inspect the new house, chattering about the wonderful new country and complaining about the misery of the past six months. But Albert was quietly content to let the love and care of his family wrap him in a peacefulness that freed the thoughts which had been smothered by the strict discipline of the German *Gymnasium*.

The elder Einsteins were simple hard-working people. They did not understand this oddly quiet son of theirs who had a way of seeming to be all alone, even in a crowd of noisy friends. The boy was never outspoken and rarely expressed his feelings, but the parents' deep love for him made them realize his disturbed state of mind.

"Things must have gone badly these last few months in Munich," said his father, sighing.

"The boy is tired, Hermann. The work must have been too much for him. Wait and see. . . . A short while in this good climate . . . my wholesome food . . . he'll soon pick up."

Albert's father nodded slowly. "Yes, that's all very well. But you know, Pauline, business has not been good. We haven't the money to support a grown boy in lazy comfort. I don't ask that he earn his own living yet, but he must start thinking about his future. What will he do? What kind of career can he have? He doesn't seem suited to anything worth-while. He has no interest in the electrical shop. In fact, he seems to have no interest in anything but dreaming and reading."

"He's very good at mathematics," Mrs. Einstein offered timidly. "Wouldn't that be useful in some way?"

"Oh, yes, he is quick with figures and problems. But to be an engineer or to do any kind of technical work he needs more than just some cleverness with arithmetic. We must talk this over frankly with him and see if we can rouse his interest in something practical."

"You are right, Hermann," Mrs. Einstein agreed, but her eyes were troubled. "He must certainly think of his future. But couldn't he first have a vacation? Let's give him a little time of rest.

He's been so unhappy, and very discouraged."

So it was decided that Albert should forget about school for a little while. His parents hoped that the vacation would give him new health and energy and make him more enthusiastic for his studies.

Albert Einstein was grateful for the opportunity to be left to himself, because his thoughts were striking off in new and forceful directions. One thing was certain. He knew he could never go back to Germany. At least, not to school there. Never again would he sit in the glare of an angry professor's eyes and be bored with memorizing dates and conjugating Latin verbs. He still could not see his future clearly outlined but he determined to make the most of the calm days he was now enjoying.

Most gratifying of all was the liberty to read. At last he had the time and freedom of mind to study the books which had been tempting him for a long time. He read constantly. Wherever he went there was a book under his arm.

Maya's Italian friends liked her older brother with his calm manner and his grave face. They called him "Alberto" and invited him to join them in many of their excursions. He was never forward or boisterous, and he had an amusing way of telling little jokes and riddles. Very often he would disappear for hours and they would find him, reading, behind a sheltered rock or under a shady tree.

Walking was his greatest pleasure. To walk was to be close to nature, and his alert, eager mind noticed everything. He found interest in the smallest bud, the trickle of a waterfall, the shape of a rock, the glorious colors of sunset. He was curious about the crisscross patterns of waves on the lake when the wind was gusty. He studied the stars and the moon and wondered what was beyond them.

Man-made wonders interested him, too. He spent many hours in the Milan Cathedral with its cool and lofty interior where twenty thousand worshipers could gather at one time. He marveled that the hard, cold stone of its spires could be made to look so delicate and lacy.

In the Church of Santa Maria delle Grazie in Milan he studied "The Last Supper" which Leonardo da Vinci had painted on one of its walls.

Albert told his mother, "The painting is still beautiful, but the wonderful colors of da Vinci have faded."

"No wonder about that," she replied. "He painted 'The Last Supper' four hundred years ago! I guess a little fading can be permitted in four hundred years."

Albert shook his head. "There are many paintings, much older, whose colors are still bright and clear. Da Vinci was an experimenter; he risked using new and untried colors. He was a scientist and tried to go beyond what was already known."

Mrs. Einstein shrugged her shoulders. "People should be satisfied with things as they are. Scientist, humph!" She rustled her starched apron impatiently. "Experimenting with new things, ignoring the tried and true ways. If he'd been sensible, that painting would have been as bright today as when it was first put on the wall."

But Albert was not listening. His eyes had taken on the dreamy, faraway look that his mother knew so well. She started to tiptoe out of the room but the sound of his voice called her back.

"Mama, I believe I shall make a little tour to see more of this country. There is so much here that is beautiful and interesting."

"A tour indeed! Really! For such things we have no money, *mein Albertl.* You know Papa's business has not been going well, and . . ."

"Yes, I know that," Albert interrupted. "But I ask for nothing. I shall make a walking tour alone, sleeping outdoors and camping along the way."

He set out the next day, walking south through the Lombardy plain to Genoa, then down along the ruggedly beautiful Italian coast to Pisa. He struck off inland and roamed through the ancient villages high in the saddles of the mountains. He found Florence a place of unending delight, with all its treasures of art. From the hills around it, he spent long, thoughtful hours gazing down at the beautiful city.

This was a happy and carefree time in Albert Einstein's life. He returned to Milan rested in body and in spirit, brown and hardened from sleeping outdoors.

But bad news was waiting for him at home. Once again his father's business had failed, and the family was preparing to move to Pavia.

4. *Failure for the Dreamer*

The Einstein family was upset. In Pavia a new shop would have to be started, a new home would have to be found. There was no place for a young man, almost sixteen, who could not do his share in helping make the business a success this time.

Worst of all, there was no longer any money for further education for Albert. His parents talked to him and urged him to work toward a goal that would bring him a way of earning a living soon. They told him, "You must concentrate your efforts. . . . Be practical. . . . Think."

Of course, Albert had been thinking all along. As he walked through the beautiful Italian countryside, as he lingered in art museums, as he watched the sparkling lakes and blue skies—always he had been thinking. Most of his thinking led to decisions about things he would never do. He would never again go to a place where studies were forced by punishment, even if it meant that he must give up school forever. He decided he could never take part in what he called "the chase"—the chase for money, the chase for fame, the chase for personal comforts that he saw all around him. These meant nothing to him.

One of the things he considered was the possibility of teaching. He thought it might be good to teach in the way that he would like to have been taught. Teaching should be done with patience and thoughtfulness, pointing the way and helping, never drilling or forcing, and he felt he would be happy in that kind of work. But it would require certain certificates and he did not have enough training to get them. In fact, he had little in his background or experience that would fit him for any but the most commonplace work. This would have been very agreeable to him, if only the work would leave enough time to think about science.

Albert's parents knew their son well. They loved him, but their love did not blind them to his shortcomings. They realized that he could never hold to the routine of most jobs. To them he was a dreamer, careless about practical matters, unheeding of rules, and without any ambition at all.

At last it was decided that Albert should try for a career in some technical field. This seemed most reasonable because of his interest in mathematics, and because his father was in the electrical engineering business. It was true that he had no diploma from a *Gymnasium*, but his parents hoped that his unusual skill in mathematics would be the wedge to get him into a technical college. This college, at Albert's insistence, could be anywhere but Germany. The family agreed that the Swiss Federal Polytechnic University in Zurich was the place to try.

Letters were exchanged between Pavia and a well-to-do branch of the family in Switzerland, and an uncle agreed to send Albert one hundred Swiss francs a month. He did this purely from a strong sense of family responsibility, without having any idea that he was opening the door to an extraordinary career. One hundred francs amounted to less than twenty-five dollars and it was pitifully little, even in those days. But Albert could get along on it if he managed carefully.

There remained only the matter of the entrance examinations which had to be taken in Zurich. On a sunny morning Albert left for Switzerland. He was sorry to leave Italy but he looked forward to seeing the magnificent scenery of the wonderful country of the Alps. He was not yet too worried about the entrance examinations. He depended on mathematics to carry him through.

The taking of tests had always angered Albert. He resented having to memorize enormous numbers of facts so that the questions could pick at his mind here and there, just to prove that he had done his work. By the time he started his first examination, he was disturbed and tense.

The entrance tests took some time. Albert toiled over zoölogy and botany. He engaged in a battle with languages. He became more and more worried.

Only the tests in mathematics and physics gave him peace. He did them with confidence and pleasure. After that, nothing remained but to wait for the results.

He did not have to wait long. Director Herzog sent a message that he wanted to see Albert, who went to the office not daring to imagine what lay ahead.

The director lost no time and came immediately to the point. "Einstein," he said briskly, "the examinations show that you cannot be admitted as a student in this school."

Albert stood silent and unmoving. His face showed no emotion, and his eyes seemed tired. He was thinking, It happens again, again, again! I cannot come here to study, to find out the things I want to know. What keeps me out? . . . It is the verbs and the nouns that keep me out. It is the structure of a baboon's skeleton, the endless dates of endless revolutions. These are the walls that spring up to bar me.

The long silence made Director Herzog think Albert was not interested. This angered him and he raised his voice a little. "As a matter of fact, the results are so bad that it was somewhat impertinent of you to try at all."

"I'm very sorry, *Herr Direktor*," said Albert gently. There was a pause. "Thank you for your patience." He turned and walked slowly toward the door.

"Wait a minute!" The director was impressed by something in the boy's manner. He had a simple dignity that was appealing. "I should like to add that your tests in physics and mathematics rated unusually well. On the strength of these, we could admit you as a student if you would make up work in all your failing subjects. I suggest you go back to preparatory school."

Albert nodded gravely. "Yes, sir. Thank you, sir."

And as he was walking to the door, the director called after him, "Try the school in Aarau. Go back to preparatory school."

Go back to preparatory school! Go back to the misery and confinement of a *Gymnasium*, the boredom of the classes! Go back to the harsh words of arrogant teachers!

Albert told himself he would not do it. He was free now, and he could not put himself into a prison-like school again. But what choice did he have? There was no place at home for him until he could earn his living. Here in Switzerland there was no way of getting a job. He was not a citizen, nor was he fitted to do practical work of any kind.

He fought the battle within himself and bowed

to the only answer. With great reluctance, Albert journeyed to Aarau, a town about thirty-five miles from Zurich, and entered the *Gymnasium* there.

It turned out to be a good decision. For the first time in his life—and to his great surprise—Albert Einstein found that schoolwork could be pleasant. In Aarau there was no boredom, no continual drilling. There were open discussions in class, and for each subject there were different teachers who welcomed questions. Well-equipped laboratories in all the sciences were open to the students. At last Albert was able to get along with the subjects he had always disliked and it became clear that he was going to make up his failures in good time.

One of the teachers, Professor Winteler, took particular interest in the quiet young man who worked so hard. "Come home to dinner with me tonight," he said one day. "It will be good for you to be with a family for an evening." Then he smiled playfully and added, "And I have quite a family—seven children!"

As usual, Albert was shy and tried to refuse. But Professor Winteler urged him and insisted that they walk home together after classes

The evening turned out to be so pleasant that Albert was persuaded to move his things from his drab rooming house into a spare room in the big, cheery Winteler home. He fitted quickly and well into the family life. They seemed to understand the serious young man and did not mistake his shyness for unsociableness. They always respected his need for being alone.

Sometimes he would join the boys and girls in an excursion or picnic. But as always, his walks alone were to him the most satisfying things of all. It was on these solitary strolls that he could ponder on the problems of science which were already taking up most of his thoughts. The walks were his only form of exercise. He had always been timid and awkward in any type of athletic activity, and now he avoided every physical exertion except his jaunts through the Aarau countryside. His step was light and noiseless, yet he gave an impression of strength and firmness as he walked.

Albert had brought his violin to Aarau. As a youngster, he had taken music lessons but had never learned to play well because the hours of practice were just another unpleasant, grinding task. In the Winteler household there were musical evenings just as in his parents' home, and friends of the family gathered to play chamber music. Now Albert found himself drawn to the graceful beauty of Mozart sonatas, and more and more he joined the amateur group, trying to improve his skill in the light-flowing melodies. He found the same enjoyment in playing the violin as he did in his solitary walks, and these two activities remained his only real relaxation for the rest of his life.

The Wintelers and Albert Einstein remained fast friends. It was not unexpected when, a few years later, Albert's sister Maya married one of the Winteler sons.

5. *University Days*

In less than a year Albert had his diploma and at last he was ready to enter the Polytechnic University in Zurich. The whole Winteler family went to see their boarder and good friend leave. At the station, they laughed and joked with him because they knew his shyness made parting embarrassing for him.

"*Auf Wiedersehen*, Albert!" They shook hands, and then they patted him on the back and hugged him. "Come back for a visit soon, as soon as you can. . . . Good-by . . . good-by," they called as the train slowly pulled out.

Albert leaned from the window. He was smiling warmly and he raised his arm in farewell. "*Auf Wiedersehen!*"

He had come to Aarau from Italy with feelings of great insecurity. Now he was leaving in a much better state of mind. The stay in Aarau had given him more than a diploma. It had also given him a chance to find out just where his special talents lay.

In the past months he had spent every spare moment in the physics laboratories, and he had studied well the works of great physicists. Because he always hated learning by drilling, he now turned away from mathematics, partly because it required monotonous memorizing of formulas. His mind wanted to know things, to search out. His thoughts were always pushing forward, wanting to uncover some of the mysteries of nature. It became clear to him that physics must be his life interest.

But physics must rise from a strong foundation of mathematics. Later on, even after he was known as one of the greatest scientists of all time, Einstein always had experts at his side to do complicated calculations for him while he studied problems of physics.

No one could possibly have guessed that it was a future distinguished scientist who came to Zurich asking for admittance to the Polytechnic University. To the directors, he was only a rather shabbily dressed young man with a shock of unruly dark hair, solemn eyes, and slightly rounded shoulders. His manner was so reserved and his conversation so limited that he gave the impression of being rather simple. But his papers were in order, and so Albert Einstein found himself a duly enrolled student in the Polytechnic University. He was seventeen years old.

One hundred Swiss francs a month were not much to live on. To Albert, it was really only eighty francs a month because immediately he began to put aside twenty francs from each allowance check to save toward his naturalization papers. He had resolved to become a Swiss citizen as quickly as he could because he found the new country friendlier and more sympathetic than his native Germany.

In Hottingen, a section of Zurich near the University, he rented the cheapest room he could find, and the rest of his money he spent frugally in small, second-rate restaurants. Food was not important to him and he ate sparingly, often going hungry. Transportation cost him nothing, for he walked everywhere. His attitude toward clothing simplified his money problems, too. It never occurred to him to worry about his appearance, and he honestly felt that it made no difference to anyone else either.

Zurich was an important academic center—students came from all parts of the world seeking knowledge. In an atmosphere of this kind, Einstein was free to become the thinker, the searcher, the questioner, that he had to be. There were people to talk to who understood his aims, and who had aims of their own. He attended lectures only irregularly, neglecting all those which were not of real interest to him. Much of his time was spent in the physics laboratories or in studying by himself.

Einstein took no part in the social life of Zurich. He did not visit in the homes or seek to make friends. He seemed able to strike up an acquaintance only with serious and thoughtful people. Such friends found him good company; others were not interested. His sober personality did not draw people to him. There was so much he had to do and to think about that he could give no attention to anything but his work.

Only music kept its place in his life. By skipping meals now and then, he managed to save enough francs to attend an occasional concert. And his own violin gave him pleasure and provided him with a satisfying outlet for his thoughts.

No one at the Polytechnic gave any sign of suspecting that there was a very exceptional person in their midst. There were some who seemed to realize that the unassuming young man had a good mind. Professor Minkowski, who lectured on advanced mathematics, tried to persuade Einstein to attend his classes, but Einstein was not yet ready to accept the subject. Years later, it was this professor who helped the scientist with some of his most important mathematical work.

A fellow student, Marcel Grossmann, also admired Einstein and was able to give him some unexpected help. One day the two young men were in Marcel's room, surrounded by books and papers, in one of their frequent discussions about problems of science. But Albert was not himself. He was very quiet and seemed less eager than usual to put forth his ideas.

Marcel felt they were getting nowhere—the conversation was all one-sided. Finally he stood up. "I say, fellow, you're really not interested in this today. Let's continue it another time."

Albert nodded and did not answer.

Marcel was puzzled. Perhaps his friend was not well. He suggested, "Come down to the Cafe

Schweizerhof and let me get you a cup of coffee." He had an idea that Albert had not eaten lately.

They made their way to the restaurant and Marcel ordered not only coffee but meat and potatoes, which Albert ate absent-mindedly. Just to keep the talk going, Marcel mentioned casually, "Well, next week we have our examinations to face."

Albert looked up from his plate. There was a responsive spark in his eyes. "Yes, the examinations. How I dread them. Such a miserable business, examinations. Cramming and stuffing your mind with facts from books, cluttering up your thoughts. The ax hangs high and the examinations will set it free . . . to fall on me and cut me out of the Polytechnic."

Marcel was surprised. What an excited speech from his usually placid and unruffled classmate! He thought for a moment.

"Albert," he finally said, "as soon as you've finished, come back to my room with me. I want to show you something."

When they were upstairs again, Marcel asked Albert to sit down at the desk. Then he laid in front of him notebook after notebook filled with detailed, accurate notes of all the lectures—the lectures that Albert had not attended.

Albert passed in his examinations, and for the four years he was at the Polytechnic, the neat, careful notes of Marcel Grossmann helped him over the hurdles of the examinations. They spared him the misery of attending lectures on subjects which did not interest him and which he did not intend to follow. It was not just a matter of avoiding an unpleasant duty. He was already heading toward his life's work and would let nothing turn him aside from it.

In one of Albert's classes there was a dark-haired girl, a science student from Serbia. She was short—not even as high as his shoulder—and somewhat chubby. She had dark, sulky eyes and seldom smiled. Her name was Mileva Maritsch, and she soon joined the little group in their frequent discussion meetings. Although she said very little, she listened intently, and this attracted Albert Einstein to her. He found her an excellent sounding board when he wished to think aloud. He would talk and she would rest her chin in her hand and gaze at him, urging him on with an occasional remark or question.

By the time they were in the third year at the Polytechnic, Mileva and Albert announced their intention to be married immediately after graduation.

6. *Hungry Job Hunter*

The nineteenth century came to a close and the twentieth century moved in. Albert Einstein was twenty-one years old and now a citizen of Switzerland. His four years of university study were over. In those years he had not only gained knowledge in many subjects, but he had also enjoyed the freedom to work and to think that his mind needed. He had made great strides forward and enlarged his entire outlook toward science.

On the day he graduated from the Polytechnic,

a letter from his family brought him the disturbing news that he would no longer receive his allowance of a hundred francs a month.

Now Einstein was faced with hard reality. It was true that he thought very little about food, and such matters as clothing and other "frills" he regarded as too unimportant to deserve attention. But a man must eat and dress, and he must have some kind of income if he is expecting to be married. Mileva was determined that she would become Mrs. Einstein and had gone home to wait.

The natural thing for Einstein to do was to seek a place as assistant to the physics professors at the Polytechnic University. That was the usual course for a bright student who graduated and wished to continue working in his chosen field. It offered an adequate, if somewhat meager, livelihood. More important, it gave the beginner a chance to work toward becoming a professor.

Einstein quite confidently expected to receive an assistantship. His professors had always hinted that his work in physics more than qualified him for such a position. But quite suddenly there was no opening. Wherever he turned, whomever he asked, Einstein was put off. Sometimes he was turned away sharply. Sometimes there were vague promises for the future. But nothing now.

Einstein was discouraged. What could it be? He knew he was better fitted than anyone else for an assistantship. "Could it be that they regard me as a foreigner?" he pondered. "But I have my citizenship papers. I am a Swiss citizen. . . . Of course, I am a Jew, and even in this free country it may count against me."

It could have been the fact that he was a Jew that kept him out. It could have been, too, that the professors were unconsciously afraid of being overtaken by this extraordinary young man. Although Albert was modest and timid in personal affairs, he never hesitated to challenge the professors in scientific matters and his keen ideas often astounded them.

But turning him away now made no difference. In a few years, these same professors were to see the young man return by urgent invitation to take a special place at the head of their ranks.

Einstein walked the streets, answered newspaper advertisements, tracked down the slightest whisper of a vacancy anywhere. At last he found his first job. A physics teacher in a technical school in the city of Winterthur was ill, and Einstein was hired as a substitute.

His first experience as a teacher was not pleasant. When he walked into the classroom there was silence. Here and there a grin broke out on the face of a student. Many of the pupils were older than Einstein and much better dressed. Here was a chance to have some fun at the expense of this shabby simpleton, they thought. Ha! He's no professor! What a dumb donkey!

"Good morning," said Dr. Einstein timidly.

One of the boys in back snorted. Feet began to shuffle noisily. Someone threw a paper wad.

Einstein turned to the blackboard and took up a piece of chalk. He was being paid to teach physics to these boys. He would explain some problems

(Lotte Jacobi)

Young Albert Einstein with his sister Maya.

(Lotte Jacobi)

Albert Einstein during his student days.

Reporters surround him on his arrival in New York.

(United Press)

(United Press)

'rofessor Einstein explains an important mathematical step
ı the theory of relativity.

– LEFT: *Albert Einstein talks with a fellow scientist*
n a lonely beach in Belgium. (Acme)

The discoverer of relativity becomes honorary Chief "Great Relative" of the Navajo tribe. (Acme)

(United Press)

At times, the resemblance between brother and sister was very striking.

RIGHT: *The best remembered Einstein look—windblown hair, comfortable sweater.* →

A meeting of scientists in Princeton.

(Alan W. Richards)

(Alan W. Richards)

The distinguished scientist leaves the Institute, his favorite knitted cap pulled securely over his head . . .

. . . and sets off homeward, deep in thought.

(Alan W. Richards)

(United Press)

On the night of the great scientist's death, lights are kept ablaze in his study.

and they could pay attention or not, as they pleased. He began to talk, illustrating his point with a diagram. Now he was on safe ground, for when he was talking about physics he heard and saw nothing else, and nothing else mattered.

Slowly the noise died down. The low, confident voice of the teacher began to come through to the students and they found themselves listening, almost against their will. By the end of the hour, they were interested and respectful; and by the time the regular teacher returned to relieve Einstein of his job, the boys were very sorry to see him go.

Now Einstein had a few francs to continue his search, but there were days when he went hungry before another job turned up. This time it was as tutor to two boys in a boarding school at Schaffhausen. He liked the work and saw such improvement in the boys that he asked if he might take over all of their training according to his own methods. Such a request was regarded as a revolt, and the rebel tutor was dismissed at once.

He went back to Zurich and again started the weary rounds. Hunger really bothered him now, and there were times when he was weak from lack of food. He looked for any kind of work, but times were hard and there was nothing for the sickly-looking youth in ragged clothing who was not even a genuine Swiss.

He was discouraged and depressed. "This is the chase," he said to himself, "the chase that I wished never to be a part of—the chase for money, for success. I want only the simplest things—a shoemaker's job to keep me alive, no more. How I wish there were an island out in space where I could exist alone, where there were no personal necessities, where only thinking mattered."

Occasionally he saw some of his old classmates but they could do nothing for him. Then word got around to Marcel Grossmann of his friend's troubles. Marcel's father had influence in government circles and he was able to arrange an interview with the director of the patent office at Bern. Marcel lent Albert the money for train fare to the capital city of Switzerland.

Anyone else might have tried to put on a brave show, but it never occurred to Albert Einstein that he should brighten up his clothing and improve his appearance. With his suit frayed and threadbare, his bushy hair flying, he entered the director's office and took the chair pointed out to him.

Director Haller was disappointed. Young men recommended by Mr. Grossmann were usually brisk and elegant, but this one . . .

"What do you know about patents?" he asked abruptly.

Albert looked gravely at him. "Nothing at all," he answered.

Mr. Haller was taken aback. Did this man really want a job? Mr. Grossmann had said he did, and he certainly looked as though he needed one. But he did not act like the usual job-seeker—alert and eager to please. He seemed almost uninterested. Well, Mr. Grossmann had said that this man was an exceptional scientist, so . . .

"Dr. Einstein," said Mr. Haller, "when a man applies for a patent on his invention, he sends a technical report of it to this office. Usually there are drawings and plans, too. The work here is to look over the application, see if the invention is really workable, then rewrite the application in nontechnical language."

Mr. Haller stopped to see what effect his explanation was having on the young man. Einstein made no move and said nothing. Mr. Haller sighed and went on. "Could you do the type of work I have described?"

Einstein sat quietly for a moment, until Mr. Haller began to feel irritated with the silence. Then suddenly Einstein looked up. "I am sure I could do such work," he said, and he seemed so confident and his smile was so warm that the director found himself unexpectedly pleased.

They talked for some time. Then Mr. Haller said, "There are one or two further questions I must ask before I can offer you this position."

Einstein's spirits fell. Here it is again, he thought. He is going to ask if I am a native-born Swiss, or if I am a Jew.

"Are you a citizen of Switzerland?"

"Yes, sir." Albert reached into his pocket and brought out his papers. There it was in bold print: Naturalized Swiss, German-born.

"Very well."

A pause.

"I can offer you three thousand francs a year, to start at once. Is this satisfactory?"

"Yes, thank you, sir."

It would have seemed like a fortune to most struggling young scientists. But this was Albert Einstein, and so there was no flurry of excitement, no wordy expressions of gratitude. He had been offered a job and was quietly accepting it.

7. *Who Is the Patent Clerk?*

On the top floor of a four-story building in Bern, Switzerland, Albert and Mileva Einstein settled down to married life. It was a small apartment, plainly furnished, but it overlooked the beautiful river Aar, and in the distance on a clear day they could see the magnificent peaks of the Alps.

Albert was happy in his job as a clerk in the patent office. Along with a number of engineers, he spent his days at a desk studying plans and outlines for inventions, and he found them of continual interest. He had to be alert to catch imitations of things already invented, and he had to be imaginative to understand what the inventor was trying to show. Almost immediately, Mr. Haller saw that his new man was a success. Einstein could get quickly and instinctively to the heart of a complicated plan. Nothing was too difficult for him to figure out, nor did he put aside anything as being too ridiculous or unworkable. Every invention that reached his desk was the work of a man with an idea, and Einstein respected it.

He soon found that he could easily finish a normal day's work in two or three hours. But he would not reveal this to Mr. Haller for the sake of his fellow clerks who worked much more slowly and laboriously. Instead, he used the time to work out problems in science that never left his thoughts. He had a file in his desk drawer and whenever anyone walked by, he would slip the paper with its scribblings into the file.

The inner force that had gripped Albert Einstein ever since he knew that physics would be his life work now became even stronger. He had a job that gave him the personal necessities of living. Outside of that, all his thoughts and efforts concentrated on certain scientific ideas that had been in the back of his mind for a long time. They were strange, new notions about light, motion and outer space. The ideas were so unusual that no name for them existed. Einstein casually began to use the word *relativity* in talking about his work, little knowing that this word would come to be a famous symbol not only in the world of science but in everyday affairs as well.

More and more, as time went on, Einstein devoted his thoughts to his Theory of Relativity. The apartment overlooking the Aar became the meeting place for several young men whose work and interest in science bound them together. There was an Italian engineer named Besso. There was Solovine, a student from Rumania, and there was Konrad Habicht, a Swiss mathematician. They were all young and full of creative ambition, and so they found it easy to agree with Einstein's new theory, even though they realized that his ideas clashed with those of respected men of science.

After Albert, Jr., was born, the young scientists arriving for their discussions had to dodge lines of diapers hanging in the hallway. Einstein often took the baby for long walks. He could think equally as well when gently pushing a baby carriage as when sitting at a desk. The pleasant-faced man patiently wheeling a sleeping infant became a familiar sight in his neighborhood.

By the time his second son, Edward, was born, Einstein was deeply involved in scientific work. His duties in the patent office were a restful change. During all his other waking hours, he wrestled in his mind with questions whose answers always seemed just out of reach. He went over the work of great scientists and found he could not agree with some of their ideas. He talked about this with Besso and Habicht and other understanding friends. They were worried about going against opinions that were held in such great respect in the scientific world.

As the months went by, Einstein's mental labors became more and more concentrated. Some scientists test ideas in laboratories. He tested his ideas only with further thinking. His great mind was his laboratory, and his work in it was stupendous. In his personal life he was placid, often careless, completely indifferent to worldly things. In his scientific life he was sureness itself, forceful and unafraid.

One day in June, 1905, a young man with straggly hair trudged into the post office in Bern and handed the clerk a thick manila envelope to be weighed and stamped. It was addressed to the scientific magazine *Annalen der Physik* in Leipzig, Germany, and was quite expensive to mail for it contained thirty sheets of paper, all closely handwritten. The young man counted out the proper number of coins and smiled wearily as he turned away.

Albert Einstein had just mailed a scientific report of the results of his thinking during the previous few years. He had set down simply and clearly the ideas he had developed about space and time and the universe. Not even he could have guessed how completely these ideas would change the path of science in the future.

It was an exhausted Einstein who mounted the stairs slowly to the apartment on the fourth floor. The children were asleep. Mileva looked at him with sullen eyes as he threw himself on the bed. She had always been ill-tempered and moody, and the years in Bern had made her belligerent and resentful about Albert's disregard of his everyday surroundings.

"You are sick," she muttered. "I will call the doctor."

"No . . . no," her husband whispered. "I'm tired, just tired. . . . Let me rest."

He had no feeling of excitement, no relaxing thought of a job finished and well done. The paper he had just mailed contained the results of years of fierce mental effort, of violent labors of the mind. The strain had used up his energy as surely as if he had been toiling in a coal mine.

Einstein stayed away from the patent office for a while, recovering from exhaustion, but his mind's activity continued for he had much more to do. He gave no thought to how his work would be accepted in the scientific world. When he had sent off his paper for publication, he knew it to be right. His studies had shown certain facts to be the truth, crystal clear in his own mind. Nothing could change that.

His Theory was published. In Berlin, in Paris, in London—all over Europe—scientists read the work with stunned amazement. Here was a radical new idea, completely different from the old beliefs. Physicists were fascinated and excited, and demanded to know who "this Einstein" was who dared to think with such boldness. In which institute did he teach? In what laboratory did he do his research? How was it they had never before heard of a man who did work like this?

"This Einstein" was an unknown patent-office clerk in Bern. Daily he went to his office where he read patent claims and slipped pieces of scribbled paper secretly into a file in his desk.

At the University of Berlin, a world-famous physicist read the relativity report and decided he must talk to its author. Professor Max von Laue boarded a train and traveled all the way to Bern. He arranged to meet Einstein in a small restaurant near the railroad station.

Professor von Laue was astonished to see the figure that rose to greet him. It was that of such a young man, barely more than a boy! But science has no special demands as to youth or age, elegance or shabbiness. The distinguished professor from Berlin and the simple patent-office clerk met and talked in perfect harmony and agreement.

Shortly afterward, Einstein was invited to speak before a conference of the greatest scientists of Europe, who were to meet in Salzburg, Austria. He was glad to go, eager to talk about his work to men like these. It was his first appearance before an important scientific group.

When he stepped onto the speaker's platform before the assembly of great scholars, his wrinkled suit hung awkwardly from his shoulders and the dark mass of his hair was a heavy fringe about his head. But as he talked, his unmistakable brilliance of mind captured his listeners. These were scientists who could realize that before them stood a young man whose mental power was the key that opened the door to some of nature's greatest mysteries. He was exploring regions where man's mind had never before ventured, and no person present at that meeting ever forgot the experience.

Einstein went back to his patent work. He liked it and had no intention of leaving it. The casual passer-by had no interest in his Theory, for in those days people in general paid very little attention to the work of scientists. Only in the scholarly world did Einstein's ideas cause flurries. In Zurich, there was consternation. This man was a graduate of the Polytechnic. Why was he not one of its professors now? It made them look ridiculous to have had him among them and to have let him go.

The University of Zurich was a smaller institution than the Polytechnic. The directors were excited about Einstein's work too and felt lucky that there happened to be an opening for an assistant professor in their department of physics. The chairman, Dr. Kleiner, offered the position to Einstein.

But there were complications. It was not possible for anyone to become a professor directly. By tradition, he must first serve a period as an assistant lecturer. For this he was not paid at all by the university but was given a fee by each student who chose to attend his lectures.

Einstein himself was quite unmoved by all the excitement his work was causing among scientists. No, he felt he could not go to Zurich right now to become an assistant lecturer. He could not afford it. He had a family to support and he felt quite content with his patent-office work. He had no ambitions for himself personally. He wanted only to be left alone, to continue working as before.

But the University of Zurich was insistent, and at last Dr. Kleiner convinced Einstein that he should become a part-time lecturer at the university at Bern. In this way, he could keep his patent-office job while preparing to become a professor in Zurich.

Albert Einstein did not find lecturing very rewarding. He was deeply interested in some new discoveries and it only distracted him to have to give lectures on the science of heat. Anyway, only two students attended regularly. One was a young telegraph-office official, a self-taught man with an unusual knowledge of physics. The other was Einstein's friend Besso. These two men made a class sufficient for Einstein to be called, officially, an assistant lecturer.

The lectures were very casual matters. Einstein merely talked to his two friends, giving them his ideas on the subject. One day he arrived to find a third person in his audience—Dr. Kleiner from the University of Zurich! The young lecturer was not agitated. He conducted his talk as usual, calmly, informally, somewhat carelessly.

Dr. Kleiner was upset. This was no way for a future professor to teach. There was no dignity, no polish. He talked to Einstein afterward.

"Really, *Herr Doktor*, I must suggest that your lectures are somewhat short of what will be expected at the university. There seems to be little interest . . . only two students. Perhaps if you tried to be more stimulating . . ."

Einstein interrupted him. "You are right, Professor Kleiner. I am not good at this sort of thing. I do not ask for a professorship. I suggest you find someone else." He was not being bad-tempered or resentful. He really would have preferred not to leave his patent office.

Dr. Kleiner was disturbed and reported back to Zurich. The assistant professorship had to be filled. The only other candidate was Dr. Friedrich Adler of Vienna. But when Dr. Adler himself heard about the matter, he wrote, "Thank you for the honor of considering me for the post. However, if it is at all possible to get Einstein, I prefer not to be in competition with a man of his ability."

Albert Einstein was still in his twenties when

he was formally offered the assistant professorship at the University of Zurich, a position usually reached only after many years of working up through the ranks.

8. *An Odd Young Professor*

"And so now, Mama, your dumbhead son is going to be a real professor! Imagine such a thing!" Einstein wrote to his mother jokingly about his new job, glad to be able to tell her something pleasing instead of the usual story of failure.

He felt no personal pride about it. His only thought was that at last he could spend his full time in his chosen field of physics. Until now, the work that fired his imagination and claimed his thoughts had been done as a hobby—a side line.

He looked forward to taking his place among people who would share his interests and understand them.

In her silent, moody way, Mileva was pleased with the move. At least it meant that they could go back to Zurich. She had never been content in Bern, and hoped that life in the city of their student days might be more pleasant for her.

They had been settled only a short time when Mileva and Albert Einstein both had to adjust their ideas about their new life. Being a professor carried with it social duties which involved greater responsibilities. They had to take an apartment larger than their little attic flat in Bern, and their living expenses mounted quickly. But Einstein's salary was no greater than the one he had received at the patent office, and it meant additional scraping, trying to make ends meet.

To Einstein himself, the problems of living and getting along socially were no burden. They did not touch him at all. The deep meaning of the scientific work he was doing made all other matters seem unimportant by comparison. He no longer felt the pressure that, in his youth, had come from not being able to find out the things he needed to know. Now he had reached an inner contentment, a sureness of what he was doing. This made him more than ever removed from everyday annoyances.

With such an outlook, it was not possible for Einstein to take seriously the formalities of dress and habits that were so important to everyone else. These matters only seemed amusing to him. He laughed when Mileva suggested that he buy a new formal suit such as the other professors wore. "What a mistake it would be if the bag were more valuable than the meat inside it! No, no, elegant clothing will not improve my work in any way, my dear. I shall be more comfortable in my friendly old tweeds."

As the months went by, it became apparent that the assistant professorship was not all Einstein had hoped it would be. He had to spend a great deal of time preparing lectures, consulting with students, and doing work in the office. There seemed to be less and less of the time and solitude he needed for research. His mind was burning with eagerness to develop the new ideas that had come to him after the publication of his last scientific work when he was in Bern.

So far, his Theory of Relativity was like the framework of a house that was being constructed. It was all roughed out; the shape and outlines were clear; but there was much filling in to be done before he would consider his theory firm and complete. He began to think back with envy on his quiet days in Bern when he had wonderful, uninterrupted hours in the patent office to reflect on the work in his mind, returning at night to the little top-floor apartment with its crude furnishings and simple way of life.

Einstein's personality was completely modest. All he wanted was to be left alone so that he could continue his work. But his achievements could not be hidden and his reputation among scientists spread slowly but surely, like a creeping fire in the underbrush. Honors began to come to him from all over Europe, and many scientific organizations invited him to lecture. He accepted only a few invitations, for he was reluctant to take time away from his work for long trips.

Wherever he talked, some of the most distinguished scientists in the world came to hear him. In Paris, Madame Marie Curie left her laboratory to listen to the words of the new professor from Zurich. When Einstein spoke in Brussels, Max Planck, the leading physicist of the time, was in the audience. Professor Planck and Albert Einstein had a long discussion after the lecture. The tall, dignified German aristocrat and the tousle-haired young man in the worn tweed suit talked earnestly together with great satisfaction. They were equal brothers in the world of their thoughts.

This was the beginning of the world-wide fame that came to Albert Einstein and was to haunt him for the rest of his life. As yet it was only the people of science who knew about his work, and they sought him out only because of real interest and respect. The rest of the world was still to hear of this man.

Einstein had not been at Zurich very long when the University of Prague offered him a full professorship. Without hesitation, Einstein accepted. The post promised more freedom from routine duties and, in addition, the salary was larger, which meant that his family would be more comfortable. The University of Prague was one of the oldest in Europe and on its staff were learned men in all fields of study. Serious students came from all over the world to work in its scholarly atmosphere.

The move to Prague was easier than the move to Zurich. The Einsteins were more experienced now and knew what to expect. Yet they had barely been settled before Albert Einstein was told of a custom requiring each newcomer to call at the home of every member of the University faculty. To a man who scorned formalities of all kinds, this seemed rather silly. But he made out a complete list of addresses and set out good-naturedly,

setting aside one afternoon each week for the calls.

"At least I can see the sights of this beautiful city, since I must make these tiresome calls," he thought. For his first visits, he selected homes located in the most historical parts of the town. He plodded through Prague, enjoying the romantic landmarks and absorbing the picturesque flavor of the old city. When he had seen everything that interested him, he suddenly stopped making the calls.

The professors whom he neglected to visit were puzzled and disturbed. They had no way of knowing that Professor Einstein did not come to call simply because they happened to live in an uninteresting section of the city. Their families fretted when Einstein failed to turn up. He already had some measure of fame, and even now had a reputation for being different, so they were curious to meet him, eager to be able to say that the rising young scientist had been a guest in their homes.

In spite of many distractions, Einstein continued his own research while carrying on his full duties as a teaching professor. In the laboratory of his thoughts, the clock did not exist. His creative mind could shut out everything around him, and he could work wherever he happened to be, whether strolling through the park, sitting at his desk at the University, or rocking a crying child to sleep. His powers of concentration were enormous.

At first his students were reluctant to ask him for help. They stood in awe of this mild-mannered young professor who seemed to be very far away when he was deep in thought, unconscious of any activity around him.

But he told his students, "Please interrupt me whenever you like. All my work is up here," he smiled and tapped his head, "and the moment you leave I can go back to where it is patiently waiting."

Offers came to him from universities in other parts of Europe but Einstein felt there would be no point in changing one post for another. He was becoming uneasy about political conditions, and there were some parts of Europe where he knew he would not be able to work with freedom. The small wars that were being fought in the Balkan countries threatened to break out into a world war. The new German Emperor, William II, was an unstable monarch who built up a huge army and navy and began to demand colonies. Other European countries became very uneasy at the warlike actions of the new Germany.

Prague was affected by the unrest in central Europe and Einstein sensed that peace was threatened. He hated violence of any kind and it grieved him to know that people could not settle their differences without using force.

Then his old school, the Federal Polytechnic, offered him a position as full professor. He talked it over with Mileva. "This invitation only confuses matters," he said to her. "There would be no reason to move back to Zurich now. I am content enough here and can do my work."

Mileva's eyes flashed. "I'm glad to have this offer . . . glad. I would like to leave this musty old city."

"But you could be happy here! You have everything you need."

"I will never be happy here. I will never be happy anywhere, except in Zurich, the only city where I had any peace."

Einstein sighed. "But we are scarcely settled here. . . ."

"I want to go back to Zurich!" Mileva's thin lips closed tightly on the words as she flounced out of the room.

Albert Einstein told the authorities at the University of Prague that he would leave at the end of the summer semester of 1912. Again the Einsteins—Albert, Mileva, young Albert and Edward—packed their household belongings and moved back to Zurich.

When he left, Einstein did not realize that he was leaving behind him a small corner of confusion in the State office. Any employee leaving the country had to fill out a complicated form. With his usual disregard for formalities, Einstein did not do this. Many years later when he returned to Prague as a world-famous figure to give a special lecture, a colleague laughingly told him about the file marked "Einstein–Unfinished."

"My, my," Einstein smiled, "I must certainly set that right. The clerk must be freed of his worries immediately!" While many notables waited for him, Einstein went to the State office, completed the form, and watched with satisfaction as the clerk stamped the file, "Einstein–Finished."

If Einstein had a twinkle in his eye when he returned to his old school as a star member of its faculty, it would have been understandable. The same professors who had scolded him for being slow and inattentive and had refused to give him a beginner's job now bowed humbly as he passed them in the halls.

But the scientist had no thought for such unimportant matters. He was deeply involved in new developments in his Theory of Relativity. During his stay in Prague he had published further results which had excited the interest of scientists more than ever. Still there was much to be done. Physicists were staggered at the amazing ideas that came from this man, but Einstein himself was aware only of the new research that drew him onward.

He gained an unexpected helper in Zurich. Marcel Grossmann was there and the two old friends found satisfaction in working together again. Grossmann's dependable calculations saved Einstein much mathematical labor. His work went ahead intensively, and another report was published while Einstein was in Zurich.

But he was not in Zurich for long. Scarcely a year had gone by when he was offered membership in the Prussian Academy of Sciences in Berlin. This was indeed an invitation to be considered seriously. There would be no teaching or any other duties, and Einstein could give all his time to research. Nothing else would be demanded of him. Max Planck, the director of the Academy, and many other leading scientists of the world would be his associates there.

Einstein did not really want to leave Zurich. He was content there. And he had unhappy memories of his childhood in Germany which made him hesitate about returning to live there. But his work came first. Here was the opportunity to be free to do nothing but research. He had to accept it.

He had only one request to make: He must be allowed to keep his Swiss citizenship. So great was their eagerness to have Einstein come to Berlin that the directors of the Academy agreed to this. The proud Germans made an unprecedented exception—a member of the Prussian Academy would actually be a citizen of another country! But they wanted Einstein under any circumstances.

There was trouble from another source. "I will never leave Zurich again," declared Mileva when she heard of her husband's new opportunity.

Einstein tried to reason with her. "You *must* understand—you are a scientist, too. You know what this opportunity means."

But it had been a long time since Mileva had

even pretended an interest in her husband's work. Her bitter nature provided no room for understanding the depth of thought which absorbed him so often, and her discontent was always present.

When the time came to leave for his new appointment, Einstein went alone. Both he and Mileva knew that she would never follow him to Berlin.

9. War Years

It was spring in the year 1914. On Unter den Linden boulevard, the heart-shaped leaves were beginning to appear on the trees which gave the broad parkway its name. The huge building of the State Library was situated on Unter den Linden, and the entire front part of the building was occupied by the Prussian Academy of Sciences. Albert Einstein paused at a large window in the conference room and gazed out at the sunshine sparkling on the building of the University of Berlin across the way.

His life here was as he had hoped it would be. He had not been long in Berlin but he was well settled. He had rented a room and had reduced his personal needs to a point where he was, for the first time, completely free to devote all of his thinking to his work.

It was different without Mileva and the boys, but Einstein's intense concentration on his work left no room for regrets. He might have been lonely, but he knew that being alone was the most vital part of his life. As a student he had always been apart from the others. As a scientist, his great mind had to work alone within the vastness of his thoughts. This lightened any feeling of loneliness, and left no room at all for irritation or vanity.

More than ever now, his appearance was neglected. What need did he have for trifles such as ties or hats or haircuts? Everyday annoyances did not reach him. His cheerful smile or deep, rumbling laugh brushed aside many unpleasant happenings that would have vexed anyone else. Here in Berlin his mind soared to its greatest heights and completion of the Theory of Relativity seemed closer.

Albert and Mileva Einstein were now permanently separated by divorce. Einstein's father had died. His mother was living with Maya, who was married to a Winteler son. Mrs. Einstein wrote, "Now that you are living in Berlin, you must visit Uncle Rudy who lives at number 5 Haberlandstrasse."

Uncle Rudy was happy that his nephew had come to Berlin. To celebrate, he gave a dinner party one night, inviting all members of the family who lived within reach. They were eager to see again this relative whom they remembered as a dreamy-eyed, listless youngster. They all made a great fuss over him, proud of their 34-year-old cousin who had taken his place at the Academy beside the most prominent scientists in the world.

Cousin Elsa was there, too. She was now a widow with two young daughters, and lived with her father in the Haberlandstrasse apartment. The gay little girl of the Munich picnics was now a mature woman, heavy-set and motherly in her ways.

It was good to spend an evening with the family. There were his favorite *Weisswürste*, the pork sausages that he loved, and later in the evening coffeecake and coffee were served.

"This is excellent," said Einstein as he munched a mouthful of the golden cake with raisins and cinnamon. "It tastes just like the ones Mama used to make."

"It ought to," laughed Elsa, "I got the recipe from Aunt Pauline!"

Einstein had brought his violin, and there was an impromptu concert. The gentle strains of Mozart flowed from his bow while one of the cousins played the piano.

When Einstein left, Elsa saw him to the door. "Let me call a carriage for you. It is late, and you have far to go."

"Ha! Never a better carriage than these two legs of mine. It's a fine evening and the walk will give me a chance to do some thinking. Good night!"

"Good night, *Albertl.* Come again soon."

Albertl! It had been a long time since he had been called that, he thought, as he strode off through the dark streets, his mind already pressing on to the problems of his work.

He came more and more often to the Haberlandstrasse apartment, and at last it was taken for granted that he would have all his meals there. This turned out to be of benefit to his health, because he thought very little about food and would eat very badly in restaurants, sometimes even skipping meals altogether unless he were reminded.

Elsa tried to see that he was properly dressed for his public appearances when he went before some important group to lecture, or when he was invited to a formal function which he could not avoid. But he was very apt to appear among a group of ceremoniously dressed dignitaries wearing his baggy tweeds, and with his shoes unshined. This was shocking to the haughty Germans who liked pompous displays and used grand titles.

Einstein never noticed such things. His attitude was exactly the same toward the scrubwoman as it was toward the mayor. If others wanted to waste time and thought on fancy clothes and formal rituals, that was all right. For himself, he wanted none of it.

All his efforts centered on research, and within a year he was able to publish an important addition to his Theory of Relativity. Ordinarily this would have created a stir even greater than the one after his work at Bern. But something else had happened that absorbed the attention of the world. Germany had invaded its neighbors, Belgium and France. The First World War broke out in full fury.

Einstein, who hated war with all his being, was now living in the capital city of a nation at war. He was helpless in such a situation, and he buried himself more than ever in his work, withdrawing completely from any public activity. One day, he and Elsa were quietly married, and they took an apartment for themselves and the two girls in the Haberlandstrasse building.

People everywhere were aghast at the death and destruction caused by this terrible war. Leading Germans self-consciously tried to show that it was not Germany's fault at all. They gathered their best artists and scientists and had them sign a statement approving Germany's military actions and declaring their country innocent of any war crimes.

Ninety-two persons signed. Einstein would have nothing to do with the paper. "Too late now to seek to place the blame," he told them. "Better use your efforts to try to bring about peace again."

The officials were stunned. Up to now they had considered Einstein their prize property. They thought they had the most famous scientist in the world on their side. But Einstein believed with all his heart that war was unnecessary and inhuman, and said, "I would rather be smitten to shreds than take part in such doings."

The Germans began to look upon him with

great suspicion. Now they had three good reasons for pinning their dislike on him. He did not approve of their war, he was a "foreigner" in their midst, and he was a Jew. They would have liked to label him "traitor," too, but he was not a legal German at all. He had wisely kept his Swiss citizenship.

The Swiss people had always been glad that Einstein had chosen to remain one of them, and they did not forget him now that war was raging. Regularly they sent packages of food, and Elsa was grateful. In Berlin, food was not only very difficult to find but of bad quality as well. Elsa struggled hard to give her husband meals that would keep up his health, for his stomach had been made delicate during his jobless periods in Zurich.

10. The Burden of Fame

Einstein's Theory of Relativity tells about the relationship between time and space and matter and energy. The ideas in it are so complex that only a trained scientist can hope to understand it thoroughly. Even physicists who work with these problems are sometimes perplexed and uncertain about understanding parts of the Theory. When it was published, it was such a change from accepted scientific ideas that there were many scientists who would not believe that such theories could be developed in one man's mind unless they were backed by real proof.

Real proof was possible. If Einstein's Theory were correct, the stars seen in the direction of the sun should seem to be slightly out of their true places. But how could astronomers see these stars so close to the glaring edge of the sun? The only thing to do was to wait for a total eclipse. During an eclipse, the moon moves in front of the sun, hiding it from the earth. Then, with the glare removed, the stars in the neighborhood of the sun can be seen in the darkened sky.

The war ended in 1918, and there was to be a total eclipse of the sun in March of the following year. One of the most important scientific groups in the world, the Royal Society of England, decided to send out expeditions to Africa and to Brazil, where the eclipse would be seen best. The astronomers took with them elaborate photographic equipment and hoped that there would be no clouds to prevent their seeing the eclipse during the two minutes that it would last.

Einstein had nothing to do with these plans. He was working hard, continuing his quiet routine at the Prussian Academy.

One morning, Elsa laid a package on his desk. "These are the photographs from the Royal Society's eclipse expedition," she explained. "They have just been delivered by special messenger."

"*Ach*, yes!" Einstein exclaimed as Elsa cut away the wrappings. He lifted the large photographs and stared at them, one by one. Elsa peered over his shoulder. She saw only a picture of a black disc with a furry rim of light around it, all on a background of black. It meant nothing to her and she waited for him to speak.

There was a long silence.

"Beautiful!" The word came out like a whisper. "Wonderful!"

"Yes, it is wonderful," agreed Elsa softly. "And now you have proof."

Einstein looked up at his wife questioningly. "Proof? What do you mean?"

"Why, proof that your Theory of Relativity is

correct. No longer will some of those scientists be able to question your work."

Like the rumble of a distant train, a chuckle started deep in her husband's throat and burst out in a roar of rolling laughter.

Elsa's face flushed with embarrassment. "B-b-b-but . . . you said . . . 'wonderful.' . . . I thought you would be glad for the proof. . . ."

"Proof! Proof!" Her husband continued to chuckle. "No, my dear. I never needed the proof. *They* did!"

He had always been sure. He had not been interested in the eclipse expedition or its results. He had known what the observers would find.

"Wonderful!" he murmured again, and he meant that the photographs were wonderful. He was complimenting the work of the experts, who could take pictures that showed even the pinpoint stars in the black sky.

At this point in his life, Einstein lost forever the one thing which he most desired and cherished—his privacy. His accomplishments were no longer known only to scientists. They had sparked the interest and curiosity of the whole world. Newspaper stories were written about him in every country and in countless languages. Requests for lectures flowed in from universities, women's clubs and business organizations everywhere. Babies whom he would never see were named after him. Medals were struck in his honor. Autograph collectors stopped him in the street. A manufacturer pretentiously gave the name "Relativity" to a cigar.

Sacks of mail poured into the apartment. Elsa was overcome with details and had to have help to sort and answer the letters. Einstein himself moved through it all serenely. "Do not be overwhelmed, my dear," he reassured her. "This is a passing fancy on the part of the public. In three months they will have forgotten me and my Theory, and then life can go on as before." But in this the great mind made one of its rare errors.

As time went on, Elsa learned the role that must be played as the wife of a famous man. From the mountains of mail, she selected only those letters that she felt he should read. Skillfully she turned away celebrity hunters who would have pestered her husband endlessly. She was the shield that protected him from the publicity that constantly tried to break into his private life.

Einstein continued his work, unexcited by the attention of the world. He remained unchanged in his habits and ideas. He acted as though all of this were happening to another person. He would laugh when he saw his picture in the papers. "Who is that fat-faced gentleman with the funny nose?" he would say.

He made trips to other cities to talk before scientific groups. These journeys always worried Elsa when she did not accompany him. One time she carefully packed his suitcase and warned him, "The black suit is to be worn the evening you make your speech. Now, don't forget. Put on the clean shirt, the tie—and please, please, the socks!"

"Dear little Elsa, you worry too much about unimportant matters." He smiled at her as he went off, suitcase dutifully in hand.

When he returned, Elsa unpacked the case. The suit, the shirt, the socks—everything was untouched. "Albert! You did not dress for the speech!"

"Well, my goodness . . . I guess I forgot." He smiled at her ruefully, like a naughty boy caught raiding the cookie jar. "But then, they came to hear what I had to say, and not to see whether I was fashionably dressed. Isn't that so?" Elsa shrugged her shoulders and smiled at her husband helplessly as she hung away his unworn suit.

He would never take seriously the fact that he was regarded as an important person. When the Paris Observatory invited him to talk before the most eminent French scientists, Einstein traveled in the third-class compartment of the train. On his arrival, he walked briskly the long distance to the Observatory, not knowing that he left behind him a frantic welcoming committee looking vainly for him in the first-class section of the train.

He would accept no special consideration of any kind and insisted on being treated like everyone else. One day he suggested that a fellow professor meet him on a certain bridge so that they might walk to an appointment together.

The professor was reluctant. "I may have to be a little late," he said, "so it may be best for you to go ahead without me. I would not want you to wait for me on the bridge."

"What difference would that make?" said Einstein, shrugging his shoulders. "The kind of work I do can be done anywhere. I can think about my problems on the bridge as well as at my desk."

Einstein knew that he was now in a position where his opinions had influence on the general public and he was very cautious. But he knew, too, that he had the responsibility of using his influence if it could help a good cause. A charitable organization would be sure to raise ample funds if it got permission to use his name. Many requests came to him for aid in backing new ideas, inventions, political parties, but he would lend his support only for the sake of humanity or for the sake of science.

At this time, after many years of residence in

Berlin, he decided that he must accept Prussian citizenship. He continued to live as quietly as he could, considering that the attention of the world was upon him. He worked in a book-lined room in a turret reached by a little stairway, completely separated from the apartment. As always, he enjoyed his long walks, never noticing the stares that followed him along the street. His radiant face and striking thatch of hair were well known to everyone by this time.

As the years went by, anti-Jewish feeling in Germany became greater. A few German scientists began to call the Theory of Relativity "Jewish science" and tried to attack the whole idea. Einstein was distressed—not at the attack on his Theory but because scientists could not separate science from their personal feelings. Sometimes he would attend a talk by someone disagreeing with his work. He would listen attentively, without anger, nodding occasionally, as though the speaker were tearing down the work of a complete stranger.

His trips out of Germany for special lectures

became a restful change for him. It was good to get away for a while from the unpleasant atmosphere that was developing in his own country. And it was refreshing to meet new scientists and see new countries. Wherever he went, crowds gathered to hear and see him. He was appointed a full professor at Leiden University in Holland, but he spent only a few weeks there every year lecturing to advanced students. He thoroughly enjoyed the intervals in the quiet, pleasant country among good and understanding friends.

In 1921 Einstein returned to the University of Prague for a special lecture. To avoid the confusion and disturbance of a public welcome, his arrival was not announced. He was met at the train only by Professor Philipp Frank, the man who had taken Einstein's place on the Prague faculty years before. As Professor Frank waited for the train to arrive, he recalled Einstein's quiet and unassuming personality, and wondered how the years of world-wide fame might have affected him.

The man who stepped off the train, overcoat

rumpled, battered hat on his head, a violin case in his hand, did not look at all like an international celebrity. And the warm smile and beaming eyes were the same as they had been in the past.

That night the auditorium was filled to overflowing. Many people were there who could not possibly understand what Einstein was saying, but they had come for the experience of seeing the great man.

Afterward, the president of the university invited a small group of specially selected friends to his home to meet Einstein. There were warm speeches of welcome, and then Einstein was asked to say a few words to the group.

He answered, "It would perhaps be more understandable and more enjoyable if I were to play for you instead." He brought out his violin and proceeded to play Mozart sonatas to a small and most appreciative audience.

11. *First Visit to America*

On a bleak April morning in 1921, the *S.S. Rotterdam* steamed slowly up New York bay after an uneventful crossing from Europe. Up forward, the unmoving figure of a man leaned against the rail, gazing at the Statue of Liberty as it loomed up out of the mist and slowly faded off astern as the ship swept onward.

The man wore no hat, and the wind whipped his long, gray-streaked hair back from his high, rounded forehead. The collar he wore had little wing tips, under which his tie was fastened in a bulky knot. His brown eyes rested dreamily on the Statue of Liberty as long as it was visible, and a slight smile curved his lips.

"*Albertl!*" A low voice called his name and he looked around to see his wife beckoning to him. "Come, we must go to the next deck," she said, placing her hand on his arm. "They say the reporters will want to interview you there."

Einstein nodded and turned to follow her. This was his first trip to the United States, the country whose freedom and democracy he had always admired. The captain of the *Rotterdam* had roped off a section of the deck so that the interviews could take place without interference.

As soon as the ship was made fast to the pier, the photographers and reporters rushed aboard. They crowded into the space set aside for them and began to work.

"Look this way, sir! Now that way. Please smile. Now look up, look down. Sit down, stand up. . . . Wave your hand. . . . Just one more, please. . . ."

The cameramen worked furiously, climbing to

the railing to get a better angle, kneeling, pushing one another. The man who was the center of all the attention took it calmly—smiled, nodded, waved, as he was asked. Sometimes a questioning look swept his face, and once he glanced at Elsa and whispered, "Dear Heaven! I feel like a prima donna!"

At last the photographers were content with their work and the reporters took over. They swarmed around Einstein, notebooks and pencils in hand, asking questions, scribbling busily.

"How do you like the United States?"

"But I have not seen it yet. . . ."

"How long will you remain?"

"I do not know yet. . . ."

"Can you explain the Theory of Relativity in one sentence?"

"No! . . ."

"How many people in the world can understand your theory?"

"Any physicist who studies it can understand it. . . ."

"Can you explain why so many people who do not understand such things and have no interest in scientific problems should suddenly find your work so fascinating?"

Einstein shrugged his shoulders. "Such odd reactions should be scientifically investigated to find out the true reasons. . . ."

"Why are women so excited about the Theory of Relativity?"

Einstein threw back his head and laughed. "Because women like a new fashion every year, and this year it is the fashion to be interested in Relativity. . . ."

One of the reporters turned to Elsa who hovered, as always, in the background. "Mrs. Einstein, are you an expert mathematician?"

"No, no!" She tossed her head. By now she was accustomed to turning away questions like these. "My interest in mathematics is limited to checking the household bills."

"Do you understand the Theory of Relativity?"

She wrinkled her nose and smiled. "An understanding of Relativity is not necessary for my happiness."

At last the interview was over and the Einsteins retreated to their cabin to make ready to go ashore. On the pier, they were met by an official delegation. After the formal welcoming ceremonies, they were escorted to a large, open limousine. Then a parade of cars, headed by the Einsteins' limousine, started downtown toward City Hall.

Slowly the procession moved along. The streets were crowded with people pressed shoulder to shoulder. They had waited for hours to see this man. As his car passed they screamed and waved excitedly. Office workers were wedged in the windows of the skyscrapers along the route, and they dropped bits of white paper and long streamers of ticker tape as the limousine passed below.

Einstein stood up in his car, occasionally nodding or waving. Sometimes he smiled soberly. Bits of paper became tangled in his wind-tossed hair, and streamers settled on his shoulders.

He took it all calmly. He was accustomed to facing problems that seemed to have no answer, and he felt that this violent public reception was a problem in behavior that he could not understand. He was a simple, natural person who was always happy to be received in a friendly and kindly manner. When there were wild demonstrations, he seemed to withdraw within himself, becoming one of the onlookers instead of the target. He never willingly did or said anything that would bring him public attention or applause.

At City Hall, Einstein was greeted by the mayor and presented with a key to the city to symbolize that all of New York was his host. It was the beginning of six crowded weeks of traveling, receptions, speeches. Wherever he went, tumultuous crowds greeted him. He was received by President Warren Harding in the White House at Washington. He lectured at Princeton, at Harvard, at Columbia University.

At the end of May, the night before the Einsteins were to sail for home, there was a huge farewell dinner at the Hotel Astor in New York. It was attended by many prominent American Jews, and the profits from the dinner were to go toward the building of a university in Palestine. Einstein was very much interested in the project and talked eagerly in its behalf.

He told reporters, "In Germany and in many other European countries it is difficult for a Jew to receive a good education. I hope there will sometime be a place where they can go freely and openly for this purpose."

"But you are a scientist," a reporter pointed out, "and your work does not concern itself with charities."

Einstein pointed his finger at the man. "You forget that I am also a human being. Humanity comes first, before science."

"Do you think a college education is really necessary? Cannot all useful information be found in books?"

"I myself do not burden my memory with simple facts that can be looked up in textbooks. But the true purpose of a college education is to train the mind to think. For that reason, it is priceless."

It was an exhausted but happy couple that set sail the next day. Einstein had seen the United States mainly through streamers of ticker tape, over the heads of cheering crowds of people, and through train windows. But he had seen enough to sense the precious freedom of this land. Deep in his thoughts rested the knowledge that it might someday be his home. For a long time he had seen disaster approaching in Germany, and now he knew that, if need be, America could become his refuge.

12. *Modest Celebrity*

The Einsteins did not return directly to Germany from the United States. They stopped off in London for several days so that Einstein could keep a promise to speak on Relativity at King's College.

They did not know what arrangements had been made for them except that their host was to be the distinguished Lord Haldane. A shining Rolls-Royce, its motor smoothly purring, carried them to a beautiful residence at 28 Queen Anne's Gate. As they drew up under the portico, a liveried footman sprang to the door and opened it. Einstein reached for his violin case but servants were already unloading the luggage.

After Lord Haldane had formally welcomed them, the Einsteins followed a uniformed footman up a winding staircase and then along a wide, high-ceilinged corridor. The footman opened a door and stood back for the Einsteins to precede him. Hesitantly, they stepped through the arched doorway.

This was not the bedroom they expected to see. To the two simple people, gazing around with wide eyes, it seemed that this surely must be a ballroom! But there was their luggage, looking small and unimportant in the middle of the room.

Ah . . . his violin, the instrument that gave him so much pleasure! Einstein crossed the room and picked up the violin case lovingly.

"Permit me, sir. . . ." The footman darted to his side, took the case from his hands, delicately laid it on a chair and opened it.

Einstein shot an unhappy look at Elsa. To do

something to cover her embarrassment, she reached for one of her own suitcases.

"Madam! Permit me!" The footman plucked the suitcase from her hand. "Clara will unpack, madam." He bowed to Elsa. "I will unpack your cases, sir." He bowed to Einstein.

Einstein stood defiantly in front of the cases, staring at Elsa. Elsa stood looking helplessly at the footman. The footman stood at attention, tensely alert, ready to spring at the suitcases, like a runner waiting for the starting gun.

There was a long, heavy silence. Then Einstein sank into the nearest chair and muttered to Elsa, "*Er muss fort! Ich kann es nicht leiden!*" She made soothing, clucking sounds as she turned to the unwanted footman.

"Please . . . we call you later. . . . Go now . . . thank you very much," she said in halting English.

The footman bowed. "Thank you, madam. Please ring when you desire me to return." He pointed to the bell rope and backed out, silently closing the door.

For a moment, the elegant room was enclosed in a thick silence. Then slowly the distressed expression on Einstein's face gave way to a broad grin, and suddenly hearty, rolling peals of laughter rang out. Elsa's rippling laugh joined it and the vast, gilded room seemed to become warmer with the sound of their gaiety.

Dinner that night was a magnificent affair. Many of England's notables attended: Professor Eddington, president of the Royal Society; George Bernard Shaw, the famous playwright; the Archbishop of Canterbury, and many others. The brilliant and lively conversation ranged wide and touched often on Einstein's work.

The Archbishop, who was seated next to Einstein, had been looking forward to this meeting. He had been greatly disturbed because he could not understand the Theory of Relativity. After reading several books on the subject, his confusion was even greater. He felt it was his duty as the conscientious head of the Church of England to be informed on every subject that might have any relation to religion. He believed himself to be an intelligent man, but he had not been able to begin to understand this new theory.

"Tell me, Professor Einstein," he said, "is there a connection between Relativity and religion?"

Einstein's answer was serious and direct. "None whatsoever."

The Archbishop sighed with relief. Now he need fret no longer about not understanding this terrible, baffling subject.

Next evening the lecture hall was filled to overflowing. There was some uneasiness as to how the public would receive Einstein. England was still smarting from her wounds of the war with Germany, and it was feared that some people might not welcome a German representative of science.

There was an air of hushed excitement in the audience. Little waves of buzzing and stirring went through the tightly packed crowd as Einstein and Lord Haldane sat on straight-backed chairs at one side of the platform. On the stroke of the hour, the dignified Englishman rose and walked slowly to the center of the stage. The wave of buzzing died quickly into silence, as though a fire had been quenched.

Lord Haldane looked over the large audience. Were these people hostile to the famous scientist because he was a German? Did they come to do him honor? Were they all really interested in such a difficult subject as Relativity? Or did they come to make trouble?

He began, "Tonight we have come here to give a true British welcome to a man of genius." There was a light clapping of hands and then silence. Lord Haldane quickly finished his introduction and brought his guest forward. Einstein knew there was still anti-German feeling in the country he was visiting and he sensed a coldness in the audience.

He began to speak, and his voice was so soft it scarcely reached the back rows. Everyone strained to catch his words.

He told of his happiness in being able to speak in the country which gave the world one of its greatest scientists, Sir Isaac Newton. Science knew nothing about the boundaries of countries, he went on. Science was for everyone, everywhere, and Newton himself had made discoveries for the benefit of all the world. As he paid sincere tribute to one of their own countrymen, the visitor caught the affection of the proud audience, and his warm personality seemed to brush away any bitterness.

Einstein talked about Relativity and other matters of science. He forgot himself—forgot that he was a German and that these people were English. He was a scientist talking to people who wanted to hear about science. They were won over by his brilliance of mind, and there was no unfriendly demonstration of any kind that night. Instead, his presence was a bond that helped bring the peoples of the two countries closer together.

At last the Einsteins set out across the English Channel on the last leg of their journey home. How good it was to get back to the familiar and comfortable Haberlandstrasse apartment after the long excursion to foreign countries!

The suitcases looked quite in place set down in the Einsteins' own hallway. The living room, with its tall white-curtained windows, cheerful lamps and grand piano, welcomed them. Elsa sank gratefully into the velvety cushions of the sofa. It was dusk, and the hushed semi-darkness gave her a feeling of contentment.

Then gradually she became aware of the soft music of Mozart filling the room. She looked up. Her husband had not even taken off his coat. He was sitting in his big armchair, playing his beloved violin, and in his eyes there was a faraway look of peace.

13. World Traveler

The Einsteins returned to a little center of peacefulness inside their home, but it was no refuge against the unrest that was around them in Berlin and all over Germany. The war had left the country in a shambles. There was no work to be had and unemployment was so widespread that professional men as well as laborers were begging in the streets.

The poor and broken people of formerly proud Germany would not believe that their own blunders and wickedness had caused their downfall. They did not want to blame themselves for their misery, so they looked about for scapegoats. Foremost among these were the Jews. More and more, Jews began to find it impossible to earn a living. In all branches of life and work, they felt the pressure of the growing hatred.

The world's honor and respect for Albert Einstein protected him from these aggravations for a time. But he was a Jew, and the sight of the unfair treatment of other Jews brought out his deep sympathy. For the first time in his life he formally joined the Jewish community; for the first time he tried to use his position and power to bring aid to a suffering people.

It did no good. It only had the effect of turning the anger of some of the German people against *him*, too. He received threatening letters and occasionally at his lectures someone would shout an unkind remark.

He had little money. His salary was not large and he would never accept monetary fees or gifts.

But now he was willing to appear at functions in the interest of charity, because his presence anywhere still caused great crowds to gather. One time he traveled to a town in central Germany to play in a concert given for relief of the poor. A young, inexperienced writer had been sent to report the event. While waiting for the concert to begin, he whispered nervously to the lady next to him, "Who is this Einstein who's playing tonight?" The lady was shocked to know that there was someone in Germany who had never heard of the famous scientist.

"Good heavens, don't you know? It is the great Einstein!"

"Ah, yes, of course," returned the young reporter, busily writing.

The next day the newspaper reported the successful appearance of the "great musician, Albert Einstein," and called him a musical celebrity and violin virtuoso who played with an artistry second to none.

The Haberlandstrasse apartment rang with

hearty laughter when Einstein read the account. "Violin virtuoso . . . artistry second to none . . . ha, ha, ha. . . ." He laughed until tears came to his eyes.

Einstein had been the subject of praise and admiration in stories published all over the world. He had gathered many medals, honors and awards, but he never showed these things to anyone. He often refused to look at them himself and would say he did not deserve them. It was different with the newspaper clipping telling of the concert. He carried it around with him until it was worn out. His eyes twinkled as he would say to a friend, "You think I'm a scientist, eh? Hah! I'm a famous fiddler, that's what I am!" And he would triumphantly pull out the frayed clipping, his face wrinkled with merriment.

Only a few months after his return from the United States, Einstein agreed to give a series of lectures in Japan. Elsa was glad and relieved. She would be pleased to have him out of Germany for a while, out of the surroundings that were becoming more and more hostile. Einstein himself laughed at the idea of any danger, but his wife and friends often worried about his safety as he walked through the city so deep in thought that he did not notice anything around him.

In the fall of 1922, the Einsteins sailed from Marseilles, France, for the Orient. Their Japanese ship made a leisurely trip with many stops along the way—in Egypt, in India, in China. At every port there were warm receptions and Einstein was showered with honors and gifts. The day of his arrival in Japan was declared a national holiday and the Empress herself received the Einsteins.

The people of Japan crowded his lectures, and he had a competent interpreter who translated his words for the listeners. It impressed him greatly to see the audiences sitting motionless for hours while he talked to them in a language they did not understand about a subject they did not understand.

After one lecture had dragged on for over four hours, Einstein resolved to make his next one shorter out of pity for his patient listeners. He was quite pleased when he finished in two hours. But his feeling of triumph did not last long. That evening his hosts were very quiet and looked at him reproachfully. "The people of our city feel insulted," they told him. "Your lectures in the other cities lasted four hours. To us, you spoke only two hours!"

In this colorful country, Einstein walked whereever he could to see the people, the land and the customs. He was offered a rickshaw to take him through some of the narrow streets or over rough paths, but he firmly refused. "Never would I use another human being as an animal and permit him to carry me about!"

When the Einsteins sailed from Japan after a stay of several weeks, they took with them not only the good will of the Japanese people but cases full of souvenirs and gifts, together with memories of a visit that seemed a strange dream.

Their stop in Palestine on the return voyage was the cause of a great celebration. They stayed in the house of the British High Commissioner where all activities were conducted with great ceremony. Every time His Excellency left the official residence, a cannon was fired. Squads of military guards in gaudy uniforms drilled and paraded constantly in the courtyard.

All this Einstein took in his stride. He ignored it completely and acted naturally as always. But Elsa at last became irritated. "I am only a simple housewife," she complained one day to her husband. "I don't care for all these nonsensical displays."

"Be patient, my dear," he answered soothingly. "We are on our way home."

"It's easy enough for you to be patient. You are a famous man. If *you* make a mistake in etiquette or act according to your own feelings, it is overlooked. But I am always being teased in the newspapers. Just because I'm so near-sighted, they said that by mistake I ate the green leaves of the flowers at my plate instead of my salad. Now, really!"

It was during their trip to the Orient that the

Einsteins received some electrifying news. The Swedish Academy of Science had awarded Albert Einstein the Nobel prize for physics, one of the greatest honors that can come to any scientist. All of Germany rejoiced at the news. This was the first Nobel prize given to a German since the war, and it soothed the people's humiliation over their defeat. For the moment, they overlooked the fact that Einstein was a Jew and were proud to have him receive the prize as a German.

After only a few weeks at home, Einstein again set out on a journey—this time to accept the Nobel prize from the King of Sweden. The honor itself was priceless, but added to the glory was a practical gift of about $40,000 which went along with it. Money was of small importance to Einstein since his wants were few and easily supplied. He sent the entire amount of the prize to Mileva in Switzerland to be used for the education of his sons.

Now Einstein returned to his homeland, determined to take up his work again quietly and without further interruption. He had been developing some new ideas about Relativity and he was eager to devote himself closely to this work.

14. *Good-by to Germany*

The following years were spent in Berlin, except for short excursions to neighboring countries now and then, and a visit of several weeks to South America in 1925.

Einstein became one of the main points of interest in the city of Berlin, like the *Tiergarten* and the Brandenburg Gate. One of the first stops of tourist groups was at the University of Berlin, where the travelers would peer eagerly into rooms and down corridors, hoping to catch a glimpse of the famous scientist. Sometimes the more fortunate ones would find him talking to a group of advanced students, and they would file softly into the room to listen. This did not disturb Einstein at all. He would continue his lecture just as though the room were not filled with eagerly staring people, most of whom did not even know what a physicist was. After a few minutes—giving them ample time to satisfy their curiosity—he would say, "I will now stop for a moment to give those who have no further interest in my talk a chance to leave." Then, with only his student listeners remaining, he would go on happily.

Einstein was not disturbed by the intrusion of strangers into his life. He never could understand their interest in him, but he accepted it just as he accepted his world-wide fame, which he thought was senseless, too.

Elsa not only sifted his mail for important matters, but also sorted out his visitors. Every day people tried to see him to ask for financial help, to plead for his influence on their behalf, or to request his backing for a project. People seemed to regard him as a magician—a wizard who could accomplish impossible things. Einstein helped wherever he could, but he refused to show favoritism nor would he use his influence as a threat.

Often the visitors were important people from other lands whom Einstein was obliged to see. He received them with the same friendliness and courtesy that he showed the most humble guest. Usually Elsa hovered in the background to see that the interviews did not last too long.

Musicians were always welcomed and they were sure to be asked to join in an informal concert with Einstein. Music and long walks still remained the scientist's greatest pleasures.

Shortly before his fiftieth birthday, in 1929, Einstein published some startling new scientific ideas which he had been working out over the years. They were the first steps of what he called the Unified Field Theory, and were an outgrowth of his work on Relativity.

Once again reporters came from all over the world clamoring for interviews. They were excited by the idea of dramatically presenting the new work on his fiftieth birthday. What an appealing news story this would make!

Einstein was astonished. Why should people want to know about the Unified Field Theory? They could not possibly understand it. If anything, it was even more complicated and harder to explain than the Theory of Relativity. This insistence on making an idol of him mystified Einstein more than ever.

He decided to hide from all the bustle and excitement. On his birthday, he and Elsa slipped off to a small lakeside cottage. The day was spent quietly and the birthday dinner came out of a picnic basket that Elsa had packed. Einstein, wearing old slacks and a shapeless sweater, padded about in bare feet. He thought socks were a useless discomfort and was always glad when he could discard his shoes too. All the while, messages and gifts were pouring into the Haberlandstrasse apartment, and people were storming the door and the telephone.

Einstein realized that never again would he be able to lead the life of a private citizen. From now on, every word he said, every action he took would be a matter of public interest. He was able to accept this idea and live with it because his great mind worked with such lofty creativeness that nothing else could have any importance.

Another year passed, and Einstein was invited to come to California for three months as a visiting professor at the California Institute of Technology. It was ten years since he had been in the United States and he decided to accept.

In New York on his way to the west coast, he visited Riverside Church, high on a knoll at the edge of the Hudson River. Dr. Harry Emerson Fosdick, its minister, escorted him through the beautiful structure. At the door, the two men paused and gazed at the arch over the entrance, on which were statues of the greatest scholars in the history of mankind, including Plato, Buddha,

Confucius . . . and Einstein. Then they walked slowly through the silent church, looking at each lofty window with its stained-glass images of the past.

"There are six hundred of the greatest men of history pictured here." Dr. Fosdick's low voice came softly through the stillness.

Einstein turned and looked long and silently at the memorials. ". . . And I am the only one, among all these, who is still living?"

"Yes, that is so."

The answer seemed to weigh heavily on Einstein and he bent his head with a sort of embarrassment as he trudged out of the church.

That night the Einsteins attended the opera—a treat to the man whose greatest pleasure was music. The performance was to be "Carmen," with Maria Jeritza in the leading role. As they slid into their seats in a box, a storm of applause rose throughout the house. Einstein looked around curiously—he saw that the curtain had not yet gone up.

"It is for you, *Albertl!* They are applauding for you!"

Einstein stared at Elsa, unbelieving. Why . . . why do they do this? he wondered. He was always puzzled at his unwanted fame and he never stopped protesting against it.

Reluctantly he stood up and the applause swelled to a roar. It was several minutes before the orchestra could begin the overture.

The stay in California proved to be so pleasant and Einstein accomplished so much that he accepted another invitation for the following winter. In Arizona, on the homeward trip, he was formally adopted by the Hopi Indians as a member of their tribe. There was a flurry of excitement among the Indians as they conferred about an appropriate name for their newest tribesman. "But what does he do?" they asked one another. "A chief must be named according to his work." Then someone told them he had originated the Theory of Relativity. Fine! Albert Einstein was named "Chief Great Relative."

In the spring of 1932, Einstein was in Berlin between visits to California. The country was in an upheaval. Field Marshal Hindenburg was running for the presidency of the German Republic against a man named Adolf Hitler. Hindenburg won.

There were many who believed that Hindenburg's election was a step toward bringing back the old military war machine to Germany. The German democratic state was becoming weaker and weaker. Einstein was greatly disturbed, for he felt that now the unhappy and oppressed German people would turn to the Nazi party, which was still small and not very strong.

But through the summer, conditions did not change noticeably and the time came for Einstein to prepare for his third trip to California. He had a special passport which gave him diplomatic privileges and it was sent to the Berlin office of the United States Consul to be stamped with the visa required for all travelers entering the United States from a foreign country.

On the morning before the Einsteins were to

leave, the telephone in the apartment rang. "This is the Consul's office. Please inform Professor Einstein that he must appear here this morning."

Elsa was puzzled. "What can they want?" she asked her husband. It had been a long time since anyone had ordered him around in this fashion. "At any rate, you are busy, and I will go in your place."

"Oh, no," declined Einstein. "If they telephoned me, I must go personally."

In a driving rain, he went to the Consul's office, arriving wind-blown and wet, with little trickles of water dripping from the matted strands of his hair.

A clerk indicated a chair. "Why are you going to the United States?" he asked as he opened a folder and took up his pencil.

"I go to resume work with some of your scientists," Einstein answered. Then he smiled gently. "At the invitation of your country," he added.

The clerk made some notes. "What are your political connections?"

"Political connections? I have no political connections!" Einstein ran a hand through his tangled hair. For a moment he stared in bewilderment at the clerk. Suddenly he stood up.

"I do not intend to pursue this matter further," he said in a low, firm voice. "If there is any question about granting me a visa, I prefer not to go to the United States." His step was firm and purposeful as he turned and left the office.

There was turmoil that afternoon in the American diplomatic circles of Berlin as soon as it became known that Einstein wished to cancel his trip. Couriers flew between offices, telegrams were sent, wires buzzed. The Chief Consul himself called to explain. The questions were a routine matter in issuing all visas, and Einstein had not been singled out under suspicion. The visa was being granted immediately and the passport was being returned by special messenger.

The family sat at the dinner table. Einstein's usually calm face was stern. "Why should I have to be questioned like a criminal? They know every detail of my life—it has been publicized enough!

Everybody knows exactly where I go, what I do, how I walk, what I eat. Nothing is hidden. Yet they think I may be coming to their country for some dark, underhanded dealing. If that is the way they feel, I do not wish to go to the United States!"

Nothing more was said until dinner was almost finished. Then Elsa's soft voice broke the silence. "I'm sure it was only a mistake on the part of the clerk. The poor, bungling fellow may lose his job over this because it seems to be stirring up a storm in the newspapers."

The scientist's broad forehead took on a frown and his eyes darkened. For a few moments he sat looking thoughtfully at Elsa. Then he pushed back his chair and rose. "You are right. We cannot permit a man to suffer because of my anger. Please announce to the newspapers that there will be no change in our plans. We leave for America to-morrow."

The next morning, Einstein stood at the door of his study, his overcoat carefully buttoned, his broad-brimmed black hat jammed squarely down on his head, forcing his graying fringe of hair down to his neck. His gaze wandered slowly across the room, from his desk with its bowl in which his pipe still rested, past his chair with his comfortable old sweater still flung across it, and then along the shelves laden with books from floor to ceiling.

Resolutely and slowly, without turning around again, Einstein walked downstairs and out of the door of 5 Haberlandstrasse. He was never to see it again.

15. *Fugitive to Freedom*

The United States was a big, prosperous country with freedom of thought and action, its people fun-loving, eager and full of curiosity about everything. Yet, even among the sometimes overhospitable Americans, the Einsteins found it possible to spend a quiet, pleasant winter. They had a small house near the campus and enjoyed the clear, warm, sunny days of southern California.

There were many invitations that Einstein had to refuse. He was considered a prize guest by fashionable hostesses who tried to snare him into attending their dinner parties. "Turn them down nicely, Elsa," he would say. "They are not interested in my company. They just want me for a centerpiece."

His mail was as heavy as ever, and gifts continued to come. Many of them were small–a school child sent an animal he had carved, an unemployed man sent a bit of tobacco. These gifts charmed and pleased Einstein, but there were also expensive items which he had to send back. One wealthy industrialist sent him a Guarnerius violin valued at $30,000, which was returned with a modest note: "This valuable instrument should be played by a true artist. Please forgive me–I am so used to my old violin."

The news from Germany was not good. Adolf Hitler had been appointed chancellor of the German Reich and now he had tremendous power. His storm troopers grew more daring and ruthless, and with their help he found it easy to win the next election.

In March, 1933, Hitler became dictator of Germany. Einstein, learning of this just as he was leaving California to return to Berlin, resolved that he would cut all ties with Germany.

As the eastbound train neared the end of its journey, Albert Einstein sat alone in his compartment, staring out across the New Jersey marshes at the New York City skyline looming up grayly in the distance. The door opened softly and Elsa peered in. She said in a tense voice, "Albert, the German Consul in New York boarded the train in Newark in order to talk with you. Here he is." She stepped back to let the visitor in, closing the door slowly as if reluctant to leave the two men alone.

"Ah, Dr. Schwarz," said Einstein. "It is true that you represent the German government in New York. But it is also true that you have been a personal friend of mine for a long time. Tell me frankly about the situation in Germany." His voice grew grave. "I know it would be dangerous for me to return to Berlin."

"My dear Professor," answered the Consul stiffly, his eyes avoiding Einstein's, "I have come for the express purpose of persuading you to go back to your homeland." He cleared his throat nervously and went on. "Anyone who has acted correctly need have no fear in Germany. He will be treated with justice. I urge you to return."

Einstein stood up. "I am deeply distressed at the activities of the German government and I must inform you that I will never set foot on German soil again while such brutality goes on."

Dr. Schwarz had risen also. "That is your final decision? I cannot convince you to reconsider?"

"My final decision," Einstein nodded firmly.

There was a moment of silence while Dr. Schwarz stared intently into Einstein's eyes. Then he said, "I have done my formal duty as German Consul but I have not been able to induce you to return." Suddenly he smiled. "Now, as a private person and as your friend, I will tell you that you have made a wise decision. It would not be safe for you to go back." He put out his hand to shake that of his friend.

In New York, Einstein was greeted by cheering crowds, but now the scientist did not smile readily. He had been born in Germany. The things that were happening there now made him heartsick—more so because the Jews were being singled out for the worst treatment.

He announced that he would sail for Belgium in a few days. In the meantime, he made as many appearances as he could at the public events given for the relief of the sufferers in Germany. People thronged to see the grave scientist with the noble bearing, and he told them quietly of his unfailing belief in peace and the true greatness of man.

While they were at sea en route to Europe, the Einsteins were told that the Nazi government was enraged at his public statements against them. Agents had forced their way into the Haberlandstrasse apartment and destroyed some of his belongings. His bank account was confiscated. He did not own valuable things and had never paid any attention to money. What little there was in the bank had been saved by Elsa's skillful management. He arrived in Belgium a penniless and homeless man.

The Einsteins found a small cottage in a village on the seacoast and settled there. Immediately, Einstein proceeded with his work as though there had never been an interruption. But first he sent a letter of resignation to the Prussian Academy of Sciences. He knew he would never again work there, and he did not want to give his old friend, Max Planck, the disagreeable job of having to dismiss him.

Now there was a fierce uproar in Germany. Einstein was called a traitor for leaving the Academy, even though it was well known that his life would have been worth nothing if he had returned to Berlin. German newspapers accused him of spreading lies and of being an enemy to his country, and they printed his picture with the caption, "Not Yet Hanged!"

Elsa was terrified. She knew the Nazis were ruthless. Already several good friends of the Einsteins had been cruelly murdered in Germany for no other reason than that they were Jewish. And the Nazis had a special hate for Einstein.

The scientist himself was not perturbed and kept on steadily with his work. Sometimes he went off all alone for a walk along the beach, deep in thought. Elsa was in a cold sweat until she saw the familiar figure again, plodding along in his comfortable old sweater.

The King and Queen of Belgium were good friends of Einstein's and were happy to have him in their country. They had had some enjoyable visits together in the past. They remembered with delight how he had once accepted their invitation to a musical afternoon at their country residence. He had appeared, walking down the road, dusty and wind-blown, clutching his violin under his arm. All the while, the royal motor car with two gold-braided, uniformed attendants waited in vain at the station. They had been watching for him in the first-class area but Einstein had traveled in his favorite way—third class.

Now the King and Queen were worried. They knew the Nazis would like to get their hands on Einstein, and Belgium was conveniently next door to Germany. It was their responsibility to shelter him and protect him from their menacing neighbor. The royal couple placed a twenty-four-hour guard around the cottage and, much to the scientist's dismay, a detective was ordered to follow him on all his walks.

The guards were efficient. One day his old friend from Prague, Dr. Philipp Frank, was in Belgium and decided to visit Einstein. The visitor already knew where the cottage was located and set out to walk there. As he approached the small house, he was suddenly seized from behind and there was a scuffle. One man pinned Dr. Frank's arms behind him and another searched his pockets for weapons. Then, still holding him tightly, they pushed him to the front porch of the cottage where Elsa Einstein sat in a rocking chair. She leaped to her feet, pale and trembling.

"What is the matter? . . . Who is it? . . . What has happened?"

"Don't worry, madam. We've got him all right. He's a prowler. We caught him sneaking around the grounds."

Elsa stared. "But . . . but it's our very good friend, Dr. Frank! He's no prowler!"

The men dropped their arms and glanced sheepishly at the rumpled professor. "Oh, so sorry, sir. You understand . . . we must be careful . . . sorry."

Dr. Frank smiled as he straightened his coat. He was pleased to see that his friend was so well protected.

It was becoming quite clear that Einstein could not remain in any country close to Germany. There was always the possibility of an assassin slipping across the border to try to gain for himself the triumph of "liquidating" a man who was on the Nazi blacklist.

Invitations came from many countries offering Einstein refuge and a new home where he could work in peace. The Sorbonne in Paris wanted him, and so did the University of Madrid and the University of Jerusalem. But Einstein already knew where he would go.

In Princeton, New Jersey, the Institute for Advanced Study was being organized. It was to be an unusual place, supported by gifts from a wealthy family that wanted to establish a haven where scientists could think and work undisturbed. Einstein had some time before agreed to come to the Institute for part of every year, dividing his time between Princeton and Berlin. Now he decided to emigrate permanently to the United States.

The board of trustees were delighted to learn that he would now become a full-time member of the staff at the Institute. When they asked him to name his terms, he replied, "It would seem fair if I should get the same salary I received at the Prussian Academy in Berlin." But when they heard the amount, the trustees wrote that such a small salary would not be suitable for a man of his reputation and suggested a sum considerably larger. Einstein was dismayed and rejected the offer. His protests hampered the contract arrangements until Elsa stepped in and took over the negotiations. So at last it was settled that in the fall, Albert Einstein would take up his new life in the United States.

This time his departure from Europe was quite different from the routine in the past. Arrangements were made for him with the greatest secrecy. Although he disliked to have special attention of any kind, he knew his life was in danger and he coöperated fully.

He was put on board a small boat and taken to the ocean liner waiting for him out at sea. He was calm and gentle. He acted as though this were just another quick trip to give some lectures in California and he did not look back at all.

In New York Bay, a tugboat took him off the ship and quietly brought him ashore at a secret spot where a car was waiting. Then, smoothly and safely, without fuss or excitement, Einstein was sped to Princeton. He was in his new country, in his new home.

16. Life in Princeton

Nassau Street, the main street of Princeton, New Jersey, runs right through the center of the small town. Unlike most main streets, it has store buildings on only one side. There is the usual five-and-ten-cent store with its red front, the hardware store with lawn mowers and garbage pails out in front, the busy market, and the stone-pillared bank on the most important corner. Along the other side of Nassau Street there is a tall fence of ornamental iron that marks the boundary of the Princeton University campus.

The University's parklike grounds and handsome old buildings under enormous shade trees give an air of quiet distinction to Princeton. It is different from the other small New Jersey towns. Few others have such large bookstores. There are more sweet shops than usual, where little knots of students gather for a soda and chatter. Around the corner from these is a second-hand clothing exchange where students can get cash for a jacket or a pair of trousers when money is scarce just before allowance time. The local photographer's window shows some pictures of young men, in addition to the usual ones of babies and brides. And right in the center of the display is a large portrait of Albert Einstein.

The Balt on Nassau Street was one of the favorite gathering places of the university students. One warm spring day in 1938, a man came out of The Balt, crossed Nassau Street and set off slowly across the soft green lawn of the campus. He wore an old pair of baggy slacks, rubber-soled shoes which time had molded comfortably to the shape of his feet, and a faded sweat shirt. The slight breeze ruffled his straggly gray hair as he plodded steadily along. He was eating an ice-cream cone.

Albert Einstein was cutting across the campus to his home at 112 Mercer Street. Sometimes he liked to walk home the long way from the Institute for Advanced Study. The students nodded and smiled in a friendly manner as he passed. He was a familiar figure by now and excited no special attention. Sometimes one of the professors would fall into step beside him for part of the way.

The small white house that he lived in now was not much different from the others on the pleasant street. A wisteria vine made a graceful lavender frame for the front porch, and the large window of his study overlooked a flower garden. It was a quiet house now, and he lived alone a great deal of the time, with only his secretary to see to his meals and to take care of his business affairs. Elsa had died in Princeton in 1936 and was buried in a little country cemetery near by.

In Princeton, he lived as quietly as he had always wanted to, and he found some of the privacy that was so dear to him. If cars with overcurious people slowed down when passing his house or if people along the road turned to stare, he did not seem to notice.

Every morning, whatever the weather, he would leave the house and set off on foot toward the edge of town. Gradually the houses thinned out, and the last part of the pleasant walk took him across open country to a large building set off quite by itself in a broad meadow. This was the Institute for Advanced Study.

His office was scantily furnished. When he first arrived, he was asked what equipment he would need in his office. "Well, let me see," he answered. "A blackboard and chalk. A desk, some chairs . . . pencils, paper. I guess that's all. . . . Oh, yes! And a waste basket—an extra large one."

"An extra large one . . . ?"

"Yes." Einstein smiled. "For my mistakes, you know. I make many of them."

In his office he worked sometimes alone, sometimes with one or two assistants. Occasionally he talked to a group of advanced physics students. His lifelong habits remained unchanged. He still enjoyed most his daily walks and the musical evenings in his living room with friends.

Occasionally he would attend a concert in Princeton and as he entered the auditorium and took his seat, he seemed unaware of the rustle of excitement he caused. The presence in the audience of the slightly stoop-shouldered gentleman with the imposing crown of hair seemed to electrify everyone, and it was hard for the listeners to forget him completely and devote their attention to the music.

One evening he walked to town to the local motion-picture theater. He rarely attended, but he wanted to see the film that was being shown because it was about the life of Emile Zola, the great French writer. He paid for his ticket and walked in, only to find the theater empty. He was nearly half an hour early.

"Oh, well, it's a beautiful evening," he said to

the usher. "I shall take a stroll and come back later. May I have my ticket back?"

"That's all right, sir," the usher assured him. "You will not need the ticket when you return."

Einstein hesitated. "But . . . you may not remember me. . . ."

The usher smiled at one of the most famous men in the world. "I will remember you, sir," he said.

Einstein had true modesty. In all his life, he could never accept the fact that he was different from anyone else. A well-known scientist once sat with him on a stage before a huge audience which was wildly cheering and applauding.

"Can you explain why they do this? Do you know the reason?" asked his companion.

Einstein shook his head slowly. There was a puzzled look in his eyes. "I ask myself that too—why do they do it?" he murmured.

Life in America was peaceful, but Einstein could not forget the agony of the people he had left behind in Germany. Hitler had become a savage madman. From the land of Einstein's birth came reports of almost unbelievable horror. Those who could fled from Germany through the secret underground or by small boat at night or by crawling on hands and knees through barbed wire. Many of those who escaped appealed to Einstein for help. They wrote to him for advice, for references, for financial aid, and seemed to regard him as their leader, their great general in the army of refugees.

Einstein keenly felt the suffering of the people. No one was ever refused some sort of aid, although often it was impossible for him to do as much as he would have liked. One time he recommended four x-ray technicians for a single job that was open in a hospital. He could not bear to favor one of the four and so he recommended them all.

His sister Maya came to visit him in 1939. She had been living in Italy where she felt the oppression of approaching war. She wanted to taste some of the wonderful freedom that had become so rare in Europe.

The citizens of Princeton were startled when they first saw her walking about the streets. It seemed impossible for anyone to look so much like the famous scientist. She had the same unruly gray hair, the same heavy-lidded eyes, and when she spoke it was with the same soft tones. Somehow it made people feel good to know that anyone could look so much like the genius they admired from a distance and still be an ordinary person who knew nothing at all about science.

One day, early in August of 1939, Einstein had two visitors. They, too, were refugee scientists, and they came to tell him of some startling new research that had just been done in Europe. This work pointed the way to the possibility of releasing the tremendous power locked up in the atom. It was related to some ideas that Einstein had published far back in 1905 in the *Annalen der Physik*.

Einstein sat quite motionless as he listened. He understood quickly and clearly what these men were telling him; he knew well the people who had accomplished the remarkable work.

"The Germans know about the possibilities of atomic power, Dr. Einstein," said one of the men, speaking urgently and rapidly. "But they are in such difficulties with their own affairs that they cannot spare the men or equipment for the necessary research. The United States can do it—*must* do it—before Germany does. If Germany goes ahead with work on an atomic weapon before the United States does . . ." The visitor shook his head and there was a frightened look in his eyes.

"As it is, it will take months to get a project under way here. A beginning has been made, but much more experimenting is necessary, and it must be done quickly."

Einstein was silent for a long time. Then he said, "I understand fully how vital this is. But what can I do? It is the government that must be informed."

"Yes! That is why we have come to you! We cannot reach the government, no one will listen to us. But if *you* write to President Roosevelt, he will pay attention."

"Pay attention . . . ?" He looked uncertainly at his visitors. "He will not pay attention to me. . . ."

He will not pay attention to me. He said it simply, and he believed it to be true. Again, as in many times in the past, Einstein had to be convinced of his important position in the world. The two men spoke to him a long time, earnestly, insistently. Then Einstein opened his desk drawer and took out a sheet of paper and his pen.

The letter he wrote that day to President Franklin Roosevelt marked the beginning of the atomic age. It started the wheels turning slowly, quietly, but surely.

Everything was done in great secrecy and, on the surface, life seemed to go on as usual. But there were hidden changes. Although Einstein did little direct work on the atomic project, his connection with it was important, and his safety was a matter for government concern. He would not tolerate a guard and insisted that his activities be undisturbed. He was let alone—or so it seemed.

It was not difficult to conceal from him the precautions that were taken to protect him. His routine was well established and easy to foresee.

One time he decided unexpectedly to make a quick trip to New York. "I will not be home for lunch today," he told his secretary at breakfast. "I will take the ten o'clock train to New York and return in time for dinner."

"But you should not go alone," she protested. "Let me get someone to accompany you."

"You are as bad as all the others," he said impatiently. "I do not need company. I am quite capable of making the short trip alone."

Even as he was leaving the house, his secretary reached for the telephone.

Einstein was still some distance from the Institute when he heard rapid footsteps behind him.

"Good morning, Professor Einstein." It was one of his assistants.

"Well, good morning. You seem to be in a hurry this beautiful morning."

"Yes, yes I am. You see, I must get the ten

o'clock train for New York and I have a bit of work to finish first."

"The ten o'clock train! Why, I'm taking the same train! Are you by any chance going up to Columbia University?" asked Einstein.

The assistant looked surprised. "That is exactly where I am going, Professor Einstein, and I am happy that I will have your company."

Einstein burst into a laugh. "And my secretary worried about my going alone. Wasn't she foolish?"

"Very foolish," agreed his assistant. And he smiled slyly.

17. *The Atom Bomb*

August 6, 1945. A piercing, blinding light burst suddenly over the city of Hiroshima, Japan. There was an instant of deadly silence. Then an earth-quivering shock thundered violently down, crumbling buildings to rubble and dust, tossing and crushing cars and trucks as though they were toys. In the center of the area, the blistering heat wilted all living things beyond recognition.

The blast itself was felt only in Japan, but the true meaning of what happened was quite plain even to the most distant countries of the world. The United States had discovered how to unleash atomic energy!

In the pleasant, book-lined study of his house in Princeton, Einstein sat quietly at his desk. The flowers in the garden nodded their bright colored heads as though trying to get the attention of the silent man behind the big window. The masses of green shrubbery caught glints of the summer sun, and the leaves on the trees swayed gently.

But Einstein was not seeing the peaceful summer garden. He was seeing in his thoughts the ruins brought about by the atomic bomb in Japan, and he was deeply moved. He knew that one of his own scientific ideas of many years before had opened the way for research on atomic energy. And he knew, too, that his letter to Franklin D. Roosevelt was responsible for starting the huge bomb project.

The responsibility weighed heavily on the bowed head. It was a thoughtful, weary man who sat there, hoping desperately that his influence with the people of the world would be great enough to make them realize the fearful consequences of using atomic energy wrongly, and to persuade them to turn it only to good purposes. He resolved with all his heart to urge people to heed the warning.

18. The Lost Words

". . . and so the adjunction of this condition to our system of equations means that the absolute derivative of the associated tensor density becomes zero."

The man at the front of the room spoke slowly in the special language of physicists as he marked mathematical symbols in a scraggly design on a small blackboard. The odd words were spoken so softly and with such a thick German accent that the listeners had to pay very close attention to understand them at all.

Not more than thirty people were in the audience. Several were young advanced students who clung eagerly to each word that came from the great master's lips. Most of the others were well-known scientists from the Institute itself and from neighboring universities.

Whenever Professor Einstein decided to talk on his Unified Field Theory, it was never publicly announced on the bulletin board or by mailed notices, as were the talks by other scientists at the Institute. If there had been such advance notices, the crowds of curious people would have left no room for those few who could really understand and benefit from the lecture. Instead, the word was spread cautiously through the building from office to office: "Room E at three this afternoon!" A few special telephone calls were made, and by the time three o'clock arrived the room was comfortably filled with only those who rightfully belonged there.

Einstein finished his talk, nodded to his listeners and walked out of the room. As the door closed, the silence was broken by a buzz of voices discussing the new ideas that had just been revealed.

A janitor appeared and loosened the screws that held the blackboard in place. With great care he took it down and carried it off, holding the panel at arm's length so that nothing rubbed against it. It would be sprayed to protect the chalk marks and stored carefully away. The great scientist's writing was being preserved for the future.

Meanwhile, Einstein had gone downstairs to his office. He struggled into his leather jacket and pulled on a heavy stocking-cap. It was 1955, and he had just passed his seventy-sixth birthday. Because he had not been well for some time, his doctors insisted on his wearing the cap in the early spring, while it was still cold. Anyway, he liked the cap because Maya had knitted it for him.

An assistant was waiting for him and the two set off together across the meadow, the young man suiting his step to his companion's. Einstein no longer protested at having someone walk with him or at having to wear a head covering. He realized he was not strong now, and there were many days when he did not leave the house at all.

As the two men turned into Mercer Street, a young girl came out of one of the houses and ran across the road. She waved gaily as she passed and Einstein's solemn, wrinkled face broke into a beaming smile shining with warmth and kindness as he waved in answer. She was his friend, and many times he had helped with her arithmetic homework. All the people of Princeton had great affection for this man who walked among them as a neighbor, yet was so wonderfully and awesomely set apart.

More and more Einstein worked in his own study. As the days passed he grew weaker and his doctors were worried. In the middle of April, they took him to the Princeton Hospital for special care, and he seemed to feel better. He chatted in a friendly fashion with his visitors, and was humble and apologetic about troubling the hospital staff.

Shortly after midnight on April 18th, nurse Alberta Rozsel stood at his bedside watching him breathe with great difficulty as he slept. She started for the door to summon a doctor when suddenly she heard her patient's voice mumbling some words in German, and she hurried back to the bedside. It was too late. The world's greatest scientist—the man who knew about things beyond the understanding of most people—had died.

In Albert Einstein's lifetime, everything he had said was revered and greatly valued by people everywhere. Now he had spoken for the last time, but Miss Rozsel did not understand German. What were his final words for those who idolized and honored him? No one will ever know.

Index

F

G

H

I

J

K

L

M

N

P

R

S

43